THE CALLED...
THE CHOSEN

◇◇◇

GOD HAS ALWAYS HAD A PEOPLE

KEN MCFARLAND

Cover art "Christ of the Narrow Way" by Elfred Lee.

Copyright © 2006 by
Hollis Scarbrough
Printed in the United States of America by
Review and Herald Graphics
www.thecalledthechosen.com

ISBN 13: 978-0-9799648-1-7
ISBN 10: 0-9799648-1-4

CONTENTS

It is always good to see the big picture. Many times we become trapped in our own little world with challenges and difficulties around us that seem to close in. We begin focusing on our shoelaces and the little things around us rather than looking up and beyond the horizon to see a larger picture. Spiritually, we must see the big picture, as well as attend to the little needs around us. Jesus said in Luke 16:10, "He that is faithful in that which is least is faithful also in much." He also said in Luke 21:28, "Look up, and lift up your heads; for your redemption draweth nigh." Being humble and faithful in the small things of life is important, as is also seeing the big picture.

This special book—*The Called . . . The Chosen: God Has Always Had a People*—will thrill your heart as you trace God's constant hand in protecting and leading a faithful people throughout history. It will unfold to you the great controversy theme. As a Seventh-day Adventist, you will trace your roots to the very beginning of history and see the unique role that God has chosen for your church to play in these end times of earth's history. Certainly, Jesus is coming soon, and the long line of truth-believing followers of God has culminated in the heaven-borne advent movement of the Seventh-day Adventist Church. From Bible and Spirit of Prophecy indication we understand this church to be God's remnant people—His remnant church—which is to proclaim the three angels' messages with the power of the Holy Spirit, pointing people to Christ and His salvation, to repentance and Christ's righteousness, to the true worship of God, and to the soon second coming of Christ. Ponder these powerful words from the Spirit of Prophecy:

> "I am instructed to say to Seventh-day Adventists the world over, God has called us as a people to be a peculiar treasure unto Himself. He has appointed that His church on earth shall stand perfectly united in the Spirit and counsel of the Lord of hosts to the end of time"—2SM 397.

If you have ever doubted the mission and purpose of the Seventh-day Adventist Church to which you belong, doubt no longer. We have entered a period of time unlike any other in earth's history—a time when the Lord will use His people in a powerful way to proclaim the message of Revelation 14 and prepare people, through the grace of Christ, for His soon coming. Your church has been called to do that. You have been called by God to do that. *The Called . . . The Chosen*, written by Ken McFarland, originates with the "big picture" vision of Hollis Scarbrough and confirms the following statement:

"Seventh-day Adventists have been chosen by God as a peculiar people, separate from the world. By the great cleaver of truth He has cut them out from the quarry of the world and brought them into connection with Himself. He has made them His representatives and has called them to be ambassadors for Him in the last work of salvation. The greatest wealth of truth ever entrusted to mortals, the most solemn and fearful warnings ever sent by God to man, have been committed to them to be given to the world"—7T 138.

Can you imagine the responsibility placed by God on you and me in these momentous last days of the great controversy between Christ and Satan? This is the reason we need to be spending time in careful study of the Bible and the Spirit of Prophecy, in praying for the power of the Holy Spirit, and in sharing this wonderful message that is to be proclaimed worldwide, by God's grace. Don't ever be hesitant about your faith and the heritage of truth given us by God. This book will crystallize your conviction that Seventh-day Adventists have a divinely inspired mandate to share with the world. Consider this great challenge:

"In a special sense Seventh-day Adventists have been set in the world as watchmen and light bearers. To them has been entrusted the last warning for a perishing world. On them is shining wonderful light from the Word of God. They have been given a work of the most solemn import—the proclamation of the first, second and third angels' messages. There is no other work of so great importance. They are to allow nothing else to absorb their attention"—9T 19.

As you read this book and see how God guided His people throughout time down to the present, you will see that the Lord knew that His end-time remnant church would need special guidance from heaven. He provided the Spirit of Prophecy, which is to point us back to the Bible. He gave this for the Seventh-day Adventist Church, because this church is to be heaven's chosen vehicle to proclaim the last warning message to the world and to point people to Christ, His soon coming, and the true worship of God, which will last throughout eternity. God indicated in Revelation 12:17 that His last-day church would have two special characteristics: they would keep the commandments of God, including the Sabbath-day fourth commandment, and they would have the testimony of Jesus, which is the Spirit of Prophecy. You are part of this great movement, and as you read this book, you are reminded of that at the end of every chapter with these inspiring words: "In every age, God has always had a people—faithful and loyal, the called and chosen—and He still has a special people today."

How exciting to be part of God's people, who have the unique and happy privilege of sharing the love of God and soon return of Christ with the entire world. As Ken McFarland says in this gripping book, "You are one of the remnant messengers who know the way to get off this planet alive and have both the mission and the privilege of sharing it with others. . . . You are one of God's final chosen." May you be blessed, refreshed, energized, and Spirit-filled for mission as you read how God has led His people in the past and how He is leading us into the future and to eternal life—all through the powerful name of Jesus Christ. What a privilege to be part of this church!

Ted N. C. Wilson
General Vice President
General Conference of Seventh-day Adventists

THE GREATEST STORY EVER

This book is a story.

It's the story of the long contest between good and evil that began thousands of years ago and is not yet finished. The story of the loyal few in every century who stood bravely and firmly on the side of good. And especially, the story of those near the story's end who help to finish the great battle.

This is the story of *the called—the chosen.* The story of those God has *called* out of error and rebellion into truth and loyalty. The story of those God has *chosen* to tell the world His truth and show the world what He is really like.

Understand that this book is not an exhaustive, comprehensive history. Each chapter here touches only lightly on segments of history that other books have covered in depth. For those who desire this more detailed treatment, it is readily available in many other excellent books.

Our purpose here is instead to provide an overview—to swiftly travel through time to the present and discover how God's loyal followers today are the final links in an unbroken chain of His faithful ones from Adam onward.

This book is also not a footnoted, scholarly treatise. That isn't the form of a story. Instead, this book is personal, people-oriented, and focuses on the relationship of God and His followers.

This book is a much-abbreviated coverage of the same great story told in Ellen White's magnificent Conflict of the Ages Series. But included here is a continuation of the story chronicled there, to include the journey of God's people through the decades since that Series was written.

Lucifer and Michael, Adam and Eve, Noah, Moses, Peter and Paul, the Waldenses, Martin Luther, James and Ellen White—you'll find here all of these and many others.

Including you.

GENUINE VERSUS COUNTERFEIT

You're a Seventh-day Adventist.

And whether you grew up in the church or were baptized into it later in life, you've been taught that the Adventist Church is the chosen remnant—a movement God Himself raised up to call His true followers out of the confused Babylon of other churches.

But are you sure about this?

Are you *absolutely* sure?

After all, the *World Christian Encyclopedia* identifies 10,000 distinct religions around the world. And just one of those religions—Christianity—includes 33,830 different worldwide denominations.

Every one of those more than 33,000 denominations believes it is the one true church of God on earth. Enter the search term *true church* into the largest Internet search engine—Google— and you get back well over half a million entries.

Ask a Mormon, a Jehovah's Witness, a Roman Catholic— and each of these members will rush to assure you that theirs is the only true church on earth. So will members of every other denomination. As will members of the Jewish faith. Or the Muslim, Buddhist, or Anglican faiths.

But can everyone be right?

And if God really has a true church on earth, can you be sure yours—the Seventh-day Adventist Church—is the one?

Perhaps you long ago settled that question for yourself beyond even the shadow of a doubt. If so, the story about to be told in these pages will doubtless confirm you in your certainty. It will open to view the exact role God has called you personally to play in the great struggle between good and evil—between truth and error.

Perhaps, though, you still wrestle, at least occasionally, with this question of whether your church—the Seventh-day Adventist Church—is indeed the home of God's last-day message and chosen followers. You wonder at times if that claim isn't just a bit audacious, exclusive, even arrogant. You remember how Old Testament Israel, despite being the chosen of God and the repository of His truth, came to see itself as spiritually superior to all other nations, even as it immersed itself in their heathen and pagan practices.

If you haven't yet conclusively answered this question of the role of your Church, the story about to be told in these pages will most certainly provide you with information that will help you toward discovering your own answer.

In the mid-1950s in America, a TV game show went on the air called "To Tell the Truth." In various forms, it was on the air, then off, then on again all the way to the year 2002.

Any of you who might have seen this game show know that it featured three contestants who each claimed to be the same person—but two of them were imposters. A panel of celebrities would question the contestants and then vote for the one they thought was the "real" person.

After the vote, the host would ask the question, "Will the

real [and here, the genuine contestant's name would be inserted] please stand up?"

Today, we might well ask, "Will the real true church please stand up?"

To find the answer to that question, do we have to research the beliefs of all the world's 10,000 religions, including over 33,000 Christian groups? Thankfully, no, we don't. Who has that kind of time? And the process would lead to absolute confusion.

Here's a suggestion. Instead of studying every single religion on earth to find out which one teaches the truth, let's just go to the Bible and discover there the marks it provides for us to identify God's true church.

Instead of studying all the counterfeits, let's simply study the genuine article.

On the United States Secret Service Internet website, you can find a section called "How to detect counterfeit money." Here's what it says: "Look at the money you receive. Compare a suspect note with a genuine note of the same denomination and series...Look for differences, not similarities."

Now obviously, in order to follow this advice, you must have a genuine note of money with which to compare others. And you must know the genuine item forward and backward, inside and out.

A good Secret Service agent in the counterfeit division spends most of his or her time getting to know the genuine article—not in looking at counterfeits. Because once that's accomplished, detecting a counterfeit is the easy part.

In the pages ahead, we'll find what the Bible has to say about genuine versus counterfeit—about truth versus lies.

But every story has a beginning. So what do you say we start there?

CHAPTER 1

ONCE UPON A TIME

When you hear "Once upon a time," you know a story is coming.

When the first "Star Wars" movie appeared in 1977, it began, "A long time ago...in a galaxy far, far away"—and viewers knew a story was coming.

And then there was the story my dad once told me.

The same year that "Star Wars" hit big screens, "Roots"—a mini-series by author Alex Haley about his African ancestors—hit small screens. For several weeks, a huge television audience watched the captivating drama.

Suddenly, the study of one's "roots" spurred countless Americans to take up genealogical research—among them, my parents.

In due course, Dad wanted to share with me what he'd learned from his extensive study. So on a weekend afternoon, I drove to his place and sat back to hear him out. Settling into a chair, I prepared to hear him say something like, "Our family ancestors lived in Scotland."

But no.

"Noah had three sons," he began.

I knew a story was coming. And I knew it would be a *loooonnng* afternoon.

Now, don't let me alarm you, since this will not be an overly long book. But I too have a story to share with you. And the story I want to tell you began far earlier than the time of Noah. In fact, it began more like "Star Wars"—"a long time ago...in a place far, far away." A place called Heaven.

For the story I want to share with you in these pages is, to borrow the title of Fulton Oursler's 1949 book on the life of Christ, "the greatest story ever told."

The greatest story ever told is the story of Truth versus Lies.

It's the story of Love versus Selfishness.

It's the story of Light versus Darkness.

It's the story of Good versus Evil.

It's the story of Michael (Jesus) versus Lucifer (Satan).

It's the story of Christ's followers versus the devil's followers.

And the central theme of this book will focus on the story of those true followers of Christ, tracing their history on earth from before the Fall of human beings to the future restoration of a perfect world.

God has always had faithful followers—those loyal to His truth and committed to following His will.

God has always had those who boldly tell the truth about Him.

God has always had a people on this earth—the faithful few, the called and chosen, the defenders and proclaimers of His truth.

And God still has a people. We'll take a closer look at them in later chapters.

For now, though, let's begin at the beginning.

Come with me now, to a time that may take real effort to imagine—a time when there was no sin, no trouble, no evil. The Bible's first chapters take us back to that time long, long ago—that place far, far away. The place we call Heaven.

Here in Heaven is God's throne. From this throne, He oversees the vast universe He has created. Countless angels—brilliant, intelligent, sinless beings whom He also created—bask in the joy and love of His presence. But when God created these angels, He chose to take a great risk. You see, He wanted His created beings to love Him because they wanted to—because they *chose* to—and not because they *had* to.

So He created each angel with the awesome gift of free choice. He did not create them as if they were computers programmed to love. They were free to choose to love and obey their Creator. But that very freedom of choice meant that they also were free to choose against Him. That is the risk God took.

Reflecting His love of perfect order, each of the angels was assigned particular tasks. And the highest angel over them all was the one called Lucifer—"the shining one." Lucifer was the "covering cherub" who stood in the immediate presence of God.

"You were anointed as a guardian cherub," God said of Lucifer in Ezekiel 28:14, "for so I ordained you. You were on the holy mount of God; you walked among the fiery stones." And in verse 12: "You were the model of perfection, full of wisdom and perfect in beauty."

In perfect peace and sinlessness, the years of eternity past moved on. How long Lucifer lived in Heaven after his creation, the Bible does not tell us. Perhaps thousands of years. Perhaps millions.

But as time continued, Lucifer apparently became increasingly focused on his own beauty and wisdom. And apparently he felt that he should be elevated to an even higher position in Heaven's line of authority.

Only two other beings in Heaven stood as equals with God the Father—Jesus Christ the Son, and the Holy Spirit. Lucifer, knowing God to be fair and truthful, doubtless concluded that God would soon recognize his personal growth, qualifications, and accomplishments and promote him to a position equal with that of the Son and the Spirit.

Pride—Then a Fall

Ezekiel 28 again, verse 17: "Your heart became proud on account of your beauty, and you corrupted your wisdom because of your splendor."

"You corrupted your wisdom." In other words, Lucifer wasn't thinking straight. His judgment became distorted by a false picture of himself that he created and chose to believe. Because of his wisdom, position, and beauty, Lucifer slowly came to see himself as more important in Heaven's scheme of things than he actually was. He became proud. He became self-centered.

Pride—an exaggerated sense of one's importance—sets one up for a fall. And eventually, Lucifer did indeed fall. After his fall, God would say of him in Ezekiel 28:15: "You were blameless in your ways from the day you were created till wickedness was found in you."

And in Isaiah 14:12-14, God added these words:

"How you have fallen from heaven, O morning star, son of the dawn! . . . You said in your heart, 'I will ascend to heaven; I will raise my throne above the stars of God; I will sit enthroned on the mount of assembly, on the utmost heights of the sacred mountain. I will ascend above the tops of the clouds; I will make myself like the Most High.'"

Lucifer's promotion never came. If he were thinking clearly, he would never lose sight of the fact that God was the Creator, and Lucifer was and could ever only be, the creature. So he waited with increasing frustration in anticipation of something that could never happen.

As time passed with no indication that God was preparing for Lucifer's imminent elevation, the prince of the angels was at first puzzled, then bitterly disappointed—and finally, angered and jealous.

At this point, Lucifer could conclude only one of two things. Either the problem was with God—or it was with Lucifer. Since the problem could not possibly be with him, Lucifer reasoned, it had to be with God.

Despite all the apparent evidence to the contrary, Lucifer concluded, God was not fair, God was not just, and God was not truthful. It seemed obvious to Lucifer that by affording special honors, privileges, and authority to Jesus, the Father was playing favorites. God simply must not be as He represented Himself to be to the universe. So the guardian cherub came sincerely to believe his own false ideas about God's character—fully accepting them as true.

For an extended period, Lucifer worked to convince the angels under him that their picture of God was inaccurate—that, in fact, God was a partial, unjust, unfair liar. Finally, the dissatisfaction Lucifer sowed grew into a full-scale revolt. The Bible describes it in Revelation 12:7-9:

> "There was war in heaven, Michael [Christ] and his angels fought against the dragon [Lucifer], and the dragon and his angels fought back. But he was not strong enough, and they lost their place in heaven. The great dragon was hurled down—that ancient serpent called the devil or Satan, who leads the whole world astray. He was hurled to the earth, and his angels with him."

And Revelation 12:3, 4 says that fully one third of the angels accepted and believed Lucifer's lies.

The great battle between Christ and Lucifer—now called the devil or Satan—began. The war behind all wars—the war that would include and be the cause of every war ever fought on earth—was now raging.

But how is it that you and I are involved in this great war between God and His government of love—and Satan and his rebellion of selfishness? How did the great conflict move from angels to human beings?

Evicted from Heaven, Satan and his fellow rebels set up the headquarters of their new counter-government on the small planet called Earth and pledged themselves to everlasting hatred—and the ultimate destruction—of their own Creator.

The Bible's first book—Genesis—tells us that on this earth, God chose to create a different order of beings, not as powerful as angels but made in God's own image. On the sixth day of creation, according to Genesis 1:26, 27, God said, "Let Us make man in Our image, according to Our likeness . . . so God created man in His own image; in the image of God He created him; male and female He created them."

God created the first human beings—Adam and Eve—to have the same freedom of choice He gave to the angels. He also created a beautiful garden called Eden as the home for our first parents. God did not allow the fallen Satan to have free access to the man and woman He created. Instead, God confined him to just one tree in the center of the garden. And God warned Adam and Eve to stay away from the tree, commanding them never to eat the fruit of it.

Tragedy

Then came a tragic day that would change earth and human history forever. Let me sketch out the story for you.

Eve hadn't intended to wander away from her husband Adam. But somehow, happily preoccupied with her work, she suddenly found herself alone, looking up at the tree God earlier warned them about.

His warning returned to her mind: "You may eat the fruit from any tree in Eden, but do not eat fruit from the tree in the center of the garden. If you do, you will most certainly die."

But waiting in the tree, in the form of a serpent, was Satan himself. And through flattery, deceit, and questioning God's motives in warning Adam and Eve away from the tree, Satan enticed Eve to take the fruit of the tree and eat it.

Before the day was out, Eve had shared the fruit of the tree with Adam.

Later that same day, as Lucifer and his forces gleefully celebrated their great victory, Adam and Eve heard God calling to them in the Garden of Eden. Normally when He called, they ran gladly to meet Him. But this evening, the Bible says in Genesis 3:8 that they "hid themselves from the presence of the Lord God amongst the trees of the garden."

"Where are you?" God called to them.

"I heard your voice," Adam finally answered, "and I was afraid."

Adam—afraid of God?

Most of us alive today have a way to go yet, too, if we are ever to feel fully at ease with God again. Ever since that day in Eden, we as His created ones have often been uneasy around Him—even afraid of Him. Somehow, sin is like that. Sin brings a break in our relationship with our Maker that causes us to see Him, not as He really is, but in a totally false light.

I don't know what your picture of God is at the moment. But I do know that if you are in the least afraid of Him, angry at Him, or uneasy around Him, it is because the separation of sin is keeping you from seeing Him as He really is.

Separated from God, we begin to imagine all sorts of things about Him that simply are not true. We begin to blame Him for the pain our own sin brings us. We come to see Him as basically against us—as our stern judge or frowning Father, if not our outright enemy.

And in creating these false pictures of God, we have a lot of help. Satan, the fallen Lucifer, is constantly at work slinging mud at God's reputation to picture Him as the worst of villains. Satan is consumed with the goal of making God look bad by telling lies about Him. So when trouble invades our lives—tragedy, pain, illness, grief—he immediately presses us to put the blame on God.

But Satan's picture of God is utterly false. Far from being our condemning Judge or enemy, God is our Saviour and greatest Friend.

The proof of God's great love for the human race is on record just a few verses beyond the sad story of Adam and Eve's fall into sin. In Genesis 3:15, God is speaking to Satan, and tells him: "I will put enmity between you and the woman, and between your seed and her seed; He shall bruise your head, and you shall bruise His heel."

These words are the first Bible promise that God would somehow save the human beings He had created. He would make a way so Someone else would bear the penalty of their sin.

God would bring enmity between Satan and Eve, and between his offspring, or followers, and hers. And of Eve's offspring—her descendents—one "Seed" would arise who would bruise Satan's head, while Satan only bruised His heel. The suggestion here is of a lethal head wound in contrast to a non-lethal wound to the heel.

The Seed who would bruise Satan's head was Jesus, the Son of God. And a day would come when that promised Redeemer would take upon Himself all the sins ever committed by every person who would ever live. He would take upon Himself all the rebellion, the selfishness, the pride, of a race that had turned away from Him. And on a cross of shame, He would bear the full penalty of death. He would give His blood and His life to save Adam and Eve.

To save their descendents.

To save you.

To save me.

The war against God began with a pride-filled angel in Heaven. It moved to Earth, where humans too rebelled and went their own way. The good news is that someday soon, the war will be over—forever and fully over.

But between the outbreak of that great war and its final end, God has had—now has—and always will have—those who stand decidedly with Him, who are firmly on His side of the conflict, who are loyal even unto death, to His truth and the defense of His character.

The story of this great war is the story of those faithful followers.

Who were the first of those faithful?

Who have they been down through history?

Who are they today?

The answers to those three questions are not wrapped in secrecy.

In every age, God has ALWAYS had a people—faithful and loyal, the called and chosen—and He still has a special people today.

CHAPTER 2

CHOOSING SIDES IN THE WAR OF ALL WARS

L et's say you're a writer. You slave away long months— maybe years—on your book manuscript. Daring to dream that you've created a potential best seller, you send it off to a major publisher.

When the manuscript arrives, the editor on whose desk it lands begins scanning through it, looking to see if you've included "IT."

It?

Yes, you have good dialogue, interesting characters, colorful descriptions, and the makings of a saleable plot. But it's not long before the editor finds that IT is missing—and you get a rejection slip. What did you leave out?

Conflict.

If a story doesn't have conflict, it's dead on arrival. Conflict can take many forms. The good guy versus the bad guy. The good country versus the evil one. The heroine versus nature (a storm, a wild animal). Even the story of someone who fights an inner battle (a bad habit, the temptation to do something illegal).

Conflict is the one element in a story that's absolutely, non-negotiably essential. Why? Because just to *live* here on this earth is to face conflict. It's a fundamental reality of life on Planet Earth. In fact, you can't live through a single day without running into IT: Conflict.

▸ It could be two small schoolboys duking it out on the playground.

▸ Maybe it's a husband and wife arguing—trading harsh, bitter words.

▸ It could be two prizefighters in a ring, each intent on punching the other's lights out.

▸ It could be the shouting of TV "talking heads" generating more heat than light about politics.

▸ It is even likely that often, you're aware of a fight taking place right inside you—a fight between your good side and your not-so-good side.

But God is a God of peace, not conflict. He created a world of perfect peace—of total harmony between people. In the beginning, even the animals were at peace with one another. The utter lack of conflict is God's ideal. And the Bible makes clear that a time is coming soon when again, this earth will be a place of absolute peace.

Conflict is an intruder. An aberration. A mutation.

Conflict is the direct fruit of sin. And sin, at its lowest common denominator, is selfishness. Sin never existed until Lucifer chose to put himself first, instead of His Creator:

"How you have fallen from heaven, O morning star, son of the dawn! . . . You said in your heart,

'*I* will ascend to heaven;

'*I* will raise my throne above the stars of God;

'*I* will sit enthroned on the mount of assembly, on the utmost heights of the sacred mountain.

'*I* will ascend above the tops of the clouds;

'*I* will make myself like the Most High'"—Isaiah 14:12-14, emphasis supplied.

Lucifer developed "I" trouble—and whenever "self" is first, conflict is the result. Life becomes all about "me." Self is exalted, protected, defended, nurtured, and responds reflexively to any threat to its first-place position. And if threatened, self fights.

So, the Bible says, there was war in Heaven.

The Great Controversy between Lucifer and His Creator had begun. And this great war, which has now raged for at least 6,000 years, is the war behind all wars.

Let's say you are led blindfolded into a billionaire's private art gallery and placed only an inch or two from one of its walls. Your blindfold is removed, and you are asked to describe what you see. You reply that you see colors—a bit of yellow, a splotch of brown. You are moved back a few inches. Now you see some kind of pattern to the color. Finally, you're moved several feet back—and now you can see that you are looking at a limited-edition print of Leonardo da Vinci's famous "Mona Lisa" painting, the original of which hangs in the Louvre Museum in Paris, France.

It helps to see the big picture.

And the Great Controversy between Lucifer (now Satan) and Christ IS the big picture. Every conflict, every war, every fight on this earth is just a small part—a tiny section—of that big picture. It is one little skirmish in the great war behind all wars.

Conflict happens when "I" is made all-important.

If "I" am right, then you are wrong.

If "I" am threatened, I'll stop at nothing to protect myself.

If "I" want something, then "I" should have it—even taking it by force if need be.

Before sin (selfishness) entered the universe, conflict didn't exist. When God eradicates sin forever and recreates our earth, conflict will never exist again. It's only here temporarily in the interim.

Before sin came along, there were no "sides," as in "your side" and "my side." Before sin, all of God's created beings were *with* Him. After sin, some turned *against* Him. So for 6,000 years or more now, there have been two sides: God's side—and Satan's side.

And note well that there is no third side. Only two. And every moment of every day, every one of us can choose only one of those two sides.

Life—or death.

Good—or evil.

Light—or darkness.

Truth—or lies.

Trust—or doubt.

Love—or selfishness.

The positive—or the negative.

Christ—or Satan.

But, someone protests, in this battle between two great leaders with totally opposite principles, I choose neither one. I'm "independent." I am loyal only to myself. Let Christ and Satan fight it out—I'm not involved.

Again, let's be unmistakably clear: There are only *two* sides. And no one in the universe can remain neutral. No one can sit on the sidelines. Why? Because unless you actively choose the right side, by *default,* you are choosing the wrong one. Not to choose Christ's side in this conflict automatically places you on the other side. You see, if you try to stake out a third, independent "side," then that's all about "I" and "me." Which puts you squarely in Satan's column.

The story of the great controversy between Christ and Satan—which is the underlying story of this book—is the story of two sides in conflict. Therefore, it's the story of how people, from our first human parents, Adam and Eve—to you and me and everyone now alive—choose which side of the conflict on which to stand.

Are we with Christ—or with Satan?

Are we loyal to truth—or to lies?

Are we driven by love—or by selfishness?

It's as simple and as real as that.

Some who admire their own intellectual prowess may protest that this sounds a lot like "black-and-white thinking." They may insist that when it comes to right and wrong, truth and error, there are only shades of gray—no absolutes.

But you can't, as the Bible makes clear, serve two masters. You must choose one. Christ? Or Satan? "Choose for yourselves this day whom you will serve"—Joshua 24:15.

There *IS* such a thing as pure truth with no error in it. There *IS* such a thing as love with no selfishness in it. There *IS* such a thing as being totally loyal to God's side without playing both sides of the fence.

Shades of Gray

Mix even a small amount of black paint into a large amount of white paint, and you end up with some slight shade of gray. The more black that is added, the darker the shade becomes.

God didn't create any shades of gray. His truth has no error in it. His love has no selfishness in it. His light has no darkness in it. "God is light; in him there is no darkness *at all*"—1 John 1:5, emphasis supplied.

There is no middle ground in the great controversy. No "shades of gray" exist between good and evil, truth and error.

To compromise—to straddle the fence, play both sides—may seem possible, but it isn't. Oil and water don't mix.

The one great theme of this book is that *God has always had a people* loyal to Him and to His truth. All through history, there have been those who have chosen to be firmly on His side in the great conflict. Those who have chosen God's side have always been in the minority—and sometimes that minority has been a very small one indeed.

"Enter by the narrow gate," Jesus said, "for wide is the gate and broad is the way that leads to destruction, and there are *many* who go in by it. Because narrow is the gate and difficult is the way which leads to life, and there are *few* who find it"—Matthew 7:13, 14, emphasis supplied.

You already know the story, so there's no need to tell it again in detail. You know that God created His heavenly beings with freedom of choice, so they could serve Him because they *wanted to* and not because they *had to*. You know that Lucifer used his free choice and chose to put Himself ahead of God. You know that this led to war in Heaven and Satan's expulsion—with a third of the angels he had deceived—from Heaven. You know that God had created a perfect earth and placed on it two perfect human beings, to whom He also gave complete freedom of choice. And you know that tragically, they too made the one horrifically wrong choice that opened the floodgates of sin on our planet.

The First Leaves Turn Brown

Adam and Eve seemed doomed. They watched flowers droop and die . . . leaves turn brown, wither, and fall from the trees—and they "mourned more deeply than men now mourn over their dead"—*Patriarchs and Prophets,* p. 62. They writhed in abject misery, suddenly aware of all they had lost. They were consumed by remorse and a sense of hopelessness. One selfish choice—and now they would die and be as if they had never been.

God could have—some might argue should have—obliterated them. He had every right to let them reap what they had sown. But we know that God chose another way. He would step in and place Himself between the wrong choice and its ultimate consequence. He would give human beings—each of them—a chance to choose again.

In compassion, God outlined to Adam and Eve His plan to save them. He let them know that while they would not be spared many of the results of their selfish choice, He would save them from its most dire and ultimate natural consequence—eternal death—but at a horrifying cost to Himself.

God would give Adam and Eve a chance to choose again.

And every one of their descendents, for as long as sin would exist, would be given the same chance. The chance to choose sides. To choose love or selfishness. Truth or lies. Christ—or Satan.

We already know that Adam and Eve lived a very long time—and that they used their second chance wisely. They were now damaged and imperfect—but daily, they chose to place themselves firmly on God's side.

We also already know that immediately, their descendents began choosing sides. Adam and Eve's son Abel, as God had instructed, brought to an altar the sacrifice of a lamb, representing the saving Lamb of God who would someday pay the ultimate price for sin. His brother Cain brought to an altar the fruit of his own labor, showing that he trusted more in his own human efforts than in God's free salvation. When God accepted Abel's sacrifice but not Cain's, Cain was furious, and the first human murder happened. Cain killed Abel.

Notice now this important commentary on that terrible event—and what it means to you and to me, living here after the year 2000:

"Cain and Abel represent two classes that will exist in

the world till the close of time. One class avail themselves of the appointed sacrifice for sin; the other venture to depend upon their own merits; theirs is a sacrifice without the virtue of divine mediation, and thus it is not able to bring man into favor with God. It is only through the merits of Jesus that our transgressions can be pardoned. Those who feel no need of the blood of Christ, who feel that without divine grace they can by their own works secure the approval of God, are making the same mistake as did Cain. If they do not accept the cleansing blood, they are under condemnation. There is no other provision made whereby they can be released from the thralldom of sin.

"The class of worshipers who follow the example of Cain includes by far the greater portion of the world; for nearly every false religion has been based on the same principle—that man can depend upon his own efforts for salvation. It is claimed by some that the human race is in need, not of redemption, but of development—that it can refine, elevate, and regenerate itself. As Cain thought to secure the divine favor by an offering that lacked the blood of a sacrifice, so do these expect to exalt humanity to the divine standard, independent of the atonement. The history of Cain shows what must be the results. It shows what man will become apart from Christ. Humanity has no power to regenerate itself. It does not tend upward, toward the divine, but downward, toward the satanic. Christ is our only hope. 'There is none other name under heaven given among men, whereby we must be saved.' 'Neither is there salvation in any other.' Acts 4:12"—*Patriarchs and Prophets*, pp. 72, 73.

From the beginning, only two sides. The side Abel and his parents chose—and the side Cain chose. Christ's side—or Satan's side. The side of faith—or the side of human works. The side of obedience—or the side of stubborn self-will. The side of loyalty to God—or loyalty to self (and by extension, God's great enemy). The side of belief in the truth about God—or in the lies Satan had told about Him.

Today, those same two sides are the only ones that exist. And every living, breathing human being is given the chance to choose which side he or she will stand on.

Adam and Eve chose.

Cain and Abel chose.

Every person in times past who has ever lived has chosen.

Now, everyone on earth is making the same choice.

Which side are *you* choosing?

In every age, God has ALWAYS had a people—faithful and loyal, the called and chosen—and He still has a special people today.

CHAPTER 3

An Unbroken Line of the Loyal

Is God losing the great controversy?

Lucifer, once the highest angel of Heaven—and transformed by his own selfish choice into Satan, the devil—might by some measures seem to be winning the great war he started. Not only did he take with him from Heaven a third of the angels, he has from the beginning won to his side the great majority of human beings.

Satan chose. Adam and Eve chose—then chose again. Cain and Abel chose. From that beginning, every person ever born has faced the same choice. And today as we count up from the year 2000, the overwhelming majority of the world's 6.5 billion people are choosing against God and for His enemy.

But God's true and loyal followers have always been—and will to the end always be—a minority. The faithful few. Those who choose the narrow, upward way. Those who stand on God's side, no matter the price they must pay to do so.

The story of this book is that of the unbroken chain of God's true followers from Adam and Eve to those who choose His side today.

So let's go back now and begin tracing this story of those who chose God's side, even as most chose the side of His declared enemy.

After Abel's death, God gave Adam and Eve another son—Seth. Seth would choose loyalty to God, just as Abel—the brother he would never know—had done. Seth's descendents for several generations followed in his footsteps, choosing to follow the God who had once walked personally with their ancestor Adam. And Adam lived nearly a thousand years—long enough to pass on in person the story of his own tragic choice and to warn his many descendents about the terrible consequences that choice had brought.

Cain and his descendents, meanwhile, chose their own territory to settle in, and generation after generation, continued the rebellion against God.

But in time, the descendents of Cain and the descendents of Seth began to intermingle and intermarry. Before long, the majority of Seth's descendents abandoned their loyalty to God and chose the rebellious stance of the expanding family of Cain. Soon, the majority of human beings were committed to the side of God's enemy.

Yet "notwithstanding the prevailing iniquity, there was a line of holy men who, elevated and ennobled by communion with God, lived as in the companionship of heaven"—*Patriarchs and Prophets,* p. 84.

A line of holy men.

A line that began with Adam and Eve.

A line that would continue, unbroken, down the centuries, for 6,000 years.

A line that can still be found today.

In that line of holy men, one of the earliest, the Bible says, was Enoch—seven generations from Adam. Surrounded by a rapidly growing world population, the majority of whom openly defied God and ridiculed His truth, Enoch "walked with God." While the world's wicked majority had no use for God, Enoch was consumed with getting to know His God better.

And Enoch didn't withdraw from contact with those who had chosen against God. He didn't lock himself away in some mountain retreat to meditate and pray 24/7 and thus become "holy." No, instead he left us—we who live today immersed in an increasingly Godless world—an example of how to be *in* the world, yet not *of* it. "Enoch's walk with God was not in a trance or vision, but in all the duties of his daily life. He did not become a hermit, shutting himself entirely from the world; for he had a work to do for God in the world"—*Patriarchs and Prophets*, p. 85.

For three hundred years, Enoch pursued God with all the passion and intensity of his soul. He came to know God intimately. Then, something amazing happened.

Vanished!

"And Enoch walked with God; and he was not, for God took him"—Genesis 5:24.

Enoch was translated—taken from earth to Heaven, without ever dying—into God's immediate presence.

On earth, Enoch's presence was sorely missed, keenly felt. But through this miracle, God had some vitally important lessons to teach His followers still on earth.

"By the translation of Enoch the Lord designed to teach an important lesson. There was danger that men would yield to discouragement, because of the fearful results of Adam's sin. Many were ready to exclaim, 'What profit is it that we have feared the Lord and have kept His ordinances, since a heavy curse is resting upon the race, and death is the portion of us all?' But the instructions which God gave to Adam, and which were repeated by Seth, and exemplified by

Enoch, swept away the gloom and darkness, and gave hope to man, that as through Adam came death, so through the promised Redeemer would come life and immortality. Satan was urging upon men the belief that there was no reward for the righteous or punishment for the wicked, and that it was impossible for men to obey the divine statutes. But in the case of Enoch, God declares 'that He is, and that He is a rewarder of them that diligently seek Him.' Hebrews 11:6. He shows what He will do for those who keep His commandments. Men were taught that it is possible to obey the law of God; that even while living in the midst of the sinful and corrupt, they were able, by the grace of God, to resist temptation, and become pure and holy. They saw in his example the blessedness of such a life; and his translation was an evidence of the truth of his prophecy concerning the hereafter, with its award of joy and glory and immortal life to the obedient, and of condemnation, woe, and death to the transgressor"—*Patriarchs and Prophets,* p. 88.

So what were the key lessons of Enoch's life and ultimate translation?

▸ Enoch's translation brought hope to the faithful still on earth.

▸ It proved that the righteous *do* have a reward—just as the wicked have a final punishment.

▸ Enoch's life showed that it is possible to keep God's commands and resist temptation, even surrounded by a world of corruption and rebellion.

▸ Enoch's translation was a small example of the ultimate reward to be enjoyed by God's faithful followers in the hereafter.

These lessons were not just for Enoch's friends who were left to carry on after his translation. They are for us today. For you. For me. Choosing God's side *does* bring rewards. Now—

and in an eternity soon to begin. And Enoch's life proves that it is possible to stay loyal and obedient to God, no matter how evil the world around us becomes.

Mind you, living an obedient life isn't the result of our own willpower, effort, and determination. Let's revisit a sentence from the most recent quotation in this chapter:

"Men were taught that it is possible to obey the law of God; that even while living in the midst of the sinful and corrupt, they were able, *by the grace of God,* to resist temptation, and become pure and holy"—emphasis supplied.

Pardon and Power

God's grace. And that grace is twofold. It is *forgiveness—pardon*—for our basic sinfulness—what we *are,* as well as for the sins we commit—what we *do.*

But grace is also *power* to keep us from sinning. We need both. And since the virus of sin—of selfishness—will always lurk inside us here on earth, not to be removed till Christ's second coming, we *always will* need twofold grace. Yet God holds out to us the possibility of becoming more and more like Him as we "grow in grace"—that is, as we learn each day to depend on it more fully.

If you'd like to review the "line of the faithful," re-read the fifth chapter of Genesis. There, generation by generation, the Bible traces the direct line of God's loyal followers from Adam to Noah. In that line, you'll discover that before his translation, Enoch had a son named Methusaleh—noted as the man with the longest lifespan in all of human history. Methusaleh lived to the astounding age of 969. Methusaleh's son Lamech would become the father of Noah.

Again, there's no need to rehearse in detail the life and ministry of Noah. Any Christian school-child knows that Noah preached to a wicked world for 120 years while building an ark. The world had become evil beyond description. "Then the

Lord saw that the wickedness of man was great in the earth, and that every intent of the thoughts of his heart was *only evil continually*"—Genesis 6:5, emphasis supplied.

Before faithfulness could be totally overcome by evil, God stepped in and brought a worldwide flood that destroyed the entire evil population of the earth. The only survivors were the eight immediate members of Noah's family who entered the ark and safely rode out the flood.

Humanity would have a fresh start—a new beginning.

But even Noah and his family carried the virus of sin, so it wasn't long before some of Noah's descendents abandoned his example and teaching, choosing to turn against God and pursue their own selfish wishes. And again, these followers of Satan multiplied as they spread out over the earth.

These rebels against God descended rapidly into violence, heathenism, and the most degrading forms of immorality. Separating themselves from God's loyal followers, they settled on a vast plain and determined to build the greatest city on earth, marked by a tower so tall it would be the wonder of the world.

The great Tower of Babel began to rise into the sky. Satan— the one who, behind the scenes, incites men to rebellion and works through them to achieve his own ends—must have been smugly gratified by the progress in the city of Babel. But God has never allowed the great enemy to wage war unopposed. Before the tower could be completed, God stepped in and confused the languages of the laborers building it. Suddenly, construction was forced to a halt.

"The schemes of the Babel builders ended in shame and defeat. The monument to their pride became the memorial of their folly. Yet men are continually pursuing the same course—depending upon self, and rejecting God's law. It is the principle that Satan tried to carry out in heaven; the same that governed Cain in presenting his offering.

"There are *tower builders* in our time. Infidels construct their theories from the supposed deductions of sciences, and reject the revealed word of God. They presume to pass sentence upon God's moral government; they despise His law and boast of the sufficiency of human reason"—*Patriarchs and Prophets*, pp. 123, 124, emphasis added.

Tower builders

The tower of evolution. The tower of human reason. The tower of a science that rises higher than God's Word. The tower of a humanly devised moral code that rejects God's law. But these towers, too, will ultimately fall. The book of Revelation is emphatic: God will not allow Satan, unopposed, to finish building any new Babylon. Yes, a new Babylon rises even now, but it too will most assuredly fall.

With the Flood, the "line of the faithful" had been given a new chance to survive—and survive, it did. Genesis chapter 11 picks up the line, tracing it through Noah's son Shem through successive generations to one of the great "giants" of Old Testament faith: Abram—later to be named Abraham.

It's assumed that readers of this book know well the story of Abraham: the covenant promise God made to him that he would become the father of a "great nation." God's call to Abraham to leave everything behind and set out—not even knowing where he was going—to follow God's leading to a land God would show him. The escape of Abraham's nephew Lot from Sodom—a city so utterly committed to evil that, along with neighboring Gomorrah, God excised its cancerous presence from earth. And of course, the miraculous birth to Abraham at one hundred years of age—and his wife Sarah at ninety years of age—of a promised son, Isaac.

Isaac, in turn, would father twin sons—Jacob and Esau. And again, these sons, exercising the sovereign power of free choice given them from God, made their life decisions. Esau would rebel and place himself on the side of God's enemy. Jacob—though so clearly flawed in some important ways—would continue the line of the faithful. After a long night of wrestling with the angel—an angel who turned out to be God Himself—Jacob would be renamed Israel.

Israel's twelve sons would become the fathers of the twelve tribes of Israel. And Israel would be specially chosen of God to preserve, defend, and share with the evil world around them, the truth about God's character.

God's vision, His intention, for Israel, was breathtaking. He chose them to demonstrate to the unbelieving nations all around them the power of God's love and grace. He chose them to be the caretakers of His truth—not to hoard it, but to preserve it even as they shared it with the heathen multitudes all around them. He chose them to prepare the way for the Redeemer to rise from among them.

The line of the faithful that began with Adam and Seth—that traveled through the patriarchs Enoch and Methusaleh and Noah, Abraham and Isaac and Jacob—now arrived at an entire nation specially chosen of God to represent Him on earth.

How would they—how *did* they—rise to their destiny?

In every age, God has ALWAYS had a people—faithful and loyal, the called and chosen—and He still has a special people today.

CHAPTER 4

WINNING THE REBELS THROUGH LOVE

To put oneself in God's place—that is, to presume to have (or try to exercise) His powers and divine privileges—is blasphemy.

But it's quite another thing to put oneself in God's place, in the sense of trying to see things from His perspective. Albert Einstein once said that science is "thinking God's thoughts after Him." But we don't have to be scientists to do this.

So for a moment, put yourself in God's place. You've created a perfect universe. You've created perfect angels—and perfect human beings. And You've created them with free will—with freedom of choice.

Giving them free will guaranteed that they would serve and worship You only because they *chose* to—not because they *had* to. But giving them free will carried a risk: They could choose against You.

Tragically, that is what they do. And on Earth, as now-sinful human beings continue to multiply, the great majority of them are in rebellion against You. Despite their sinful condition, however, a faithful few choose to worship You as their Creator.

The early pillars of faith—700, 800, 900 years old—finally die. The world becomes so evil that You bring a great Flood to cleanse away the rebellious multitudes and start over with a handful of faithful followers—the immediate family of Noah.

But in time, human beings again multiply and spread out over the earth—and again, most of them turn against You.

How do You win back the rebels?

How do You reach the wicked, the ungodly, the heathen?

Do You send unfallen angels to preach to them? Do You call a few of Your faithful followers on earth to warn the stubborn evil-doers—to plead with them, preach to them, condemn their sins?

God's Idea

If the problem had been yours or mine to solve, we might well have chosen a solution such as one of these. But God had a different idea.

He would reveal Himself to the rebels. He would demonstrate to them His character of love and rely on the power of that love to draw them back to Himself.

But He wouldn't do this in person. He would do it through His loyal followers on Earth. The time had come, however, that the task of reaching an unbelieving world was simply too large for only a few. So God would commit this task not to a scattered few but to an entire nation—a nation He would choose and bless with everything they could possibly need to reveal His love to their unbelieving neighbors.

God first revealed His plan to Abraham, somewhere around 1800 B.C. Surrounded by heathenism, idolatry, and apostasy, Abram—as he was called at that time—remained faithful to God.

When Abram was 75 years of age, God spoke to him and made an amazing promise to him: "I will make you a great nation; I will bless you and make your name great; and you shall be a blessing. I will bless those who bless you, and I will curse him who curses you; and in you all the families of the earth shall be blessed"—Genesis 12:2, 3.

In addition to this great promise, God also gave Abram a command: "Get out of your country, from your family and from your father's house, to a land that I will show you"—Genesis 12:1.

Abram obeyed God. Without hesitation. Without question. "By faith Abraham obeyed when he was called to go out to the place which he would receive as an inheritance. And he went out, not knowing where he was going. By faith he dwelt in the land of promise as in a foreign country, dwelling in tents with Isaac and Jacob, the heirs with him of the same promise"—Hebrews 11:8, 9.

So it was that Abram moved from his family home in Haran to the land God showed him: Canaan.

It is not the intent of this book to trace the detailed history of Israel from the time of Abraham in 1800 B.C. to the time of Christ's life on Earth. The unbroken chain of the faithful that began with Adam and moved through the generations to Abraham continued on with Abraham's son Isaac, and Isaac's son Jacob—who became Israel. And of course, Israel's twelve sons became the founders of the twelve tribes of the nation of Israel.

As an Adventist, the chances are very good that you are already well acquainted with the long history of the Israelites: the patriarchs, the prophets, the kings, the long bondage in Egypt, the Exodus, the forty-year journey in the wilderness en route to the Promised Land, the Babylonian captivity, and the eventual division of Israel into northern and southern kingdoms.

You are likely well acquainted with the Passover and the Red Sea, with Sinai and the sanctuary, with Israel's repeated pattern of apostasy and repentance, and with the great names of Israel's history: Joseph, Moses, David, Solomon, Samuel, Daniel, and many others.

Few pursuits can be as rewarding as reviewing the history of the Jewish nation from Genesis 11 and onward—or in the books *Patriarchs and Prophets* and *Prophets and Kings*.

The focus of this chapter is not so much on Israel's history—its chronology and leaders, its dates and places, and its times of both obedience and apostasy. Instead, once again, we carry forward the story of God's loyal followers—the faithful minority who have remained true to Him from the time of Adam to the present moment.

Chosen—for a Reason

For these few paragraphs, we dwell on Israel as God's chosen—and on the reason God chose them.

God had a great purpose for the nation of Israel. He entrusted to them blessings and promises almost too breathtaking to fully apprehend. But the blessings and promises were conditional. If they obeyed Him—if they relied fully on Him to live in and through them—they would be an astonishing marvel to all other nations of the earth. If not, they would suffer defeat—even captivity—at the hands of their enemies.

We already know that only in part—and only part of the time—did Israel fulfill God's plan and purpose for them. And we already know that ultimately, they so fully rejected God—in the immediate person of Jesus—that they participated in taking the life of their Creator.

But at Israel's lowest ebb—at their times of greatest apostasy—there always remained in Israel the faithful few, the loyal, the true followers of God. So had it always been before Israel. So would it always be after Israel.

And the same choice every Israelite had to make long ago,

you and I must make today. Will we place ourselves firmly on the side of complete loyalty to our God? Will we stay true to Him even if it may sometimes seem to us that not only the rest of the world, but even too many in our own church—perhaps even our own family—turn away from Him?

To revisit God's great plan and purpose for Israel is to find again His identical purpose for His Church today—His plan for your life and mine.

And what was that purpose?

"They were to reveal the principles of His kingdom. In the midst of a fallen, wicked world they were to represent the character of God. As the Lord's vineyard they were to produce fruit altogether different from that the heathen nations. . . . It was the privilege of the Jewish nation to represent the character of God"—*Christ's Object Lessons* (COL), p. 285.

"It was God's purpose that by the revelation of His character through Israel men should be drawn unto Him"—*COL*, p. 290.

Israel's mission? The reason God had chosen them? To represent to unbelieving, rebellious nations the character of God. And as God revealed it to Moses, His character is His goodness—a goodness that includes mercy, grace, patience, truth, and forgiveness. Ultimately, all of God's goodness is found in His love.

God wanted to win back a rebellious world that had turned its back on Him. And His plan was to reach out to them through His chosen nation. His purpose was that Israel would lift up His character of love in their own lives—and that through Israel, He would love the world back to Himself.

"Through the Jewish nation it was God's purpose to impart rich blessings to all peoples. Through Israel the way was to be prepared for the diffusion of His light to the whole world. The nations of the world, through following corrupt practices, had lost the knowledge of God. Yet in His mercy God did not blot them out of existence. He purposed to give them opportunity for becoming acquainted with Him through His church"—*COL*, p. 286.

And note well just how Israel was to win the nations back to God. Was it by condemning their idolatrous, evil, heathen ways?

Something Better

All too often today, even well-known preachers publicly condemn the sins of those who live Godless lives. They threaten sinners with God's wrathful judgments. Or when natural disasters happen, they point to them as evidence of God's anger and displeasure.

Is that what God calls us to do? Is that what He called Israel to do?

"The people of the world are worshiping false gods. They are to be turned from their false worship, not by hearing denunciation of their idols, but by beholding something better. God's goodness is to be made known"—*COL*, p. 299.

Yes, those who live apart from God fall into truly abominable sins. But whether Israel of old or God's people today, is it the mission of God's followers to condemn, to denounce, to call down God's judgments?

Or is it instead to show the world something better? And what is that "something better"? God's goodness. His character. His love.

In reaching the sinful world through His followers, has it ever been God's plan to threaten the world back to Himself? To win them with anger and condemnation? To browbeat them with their sins?

Or is it not instead that God has only one way of winning

back the rebels: to show them His love so clearly that they will be irresistibly drawn back to Him.

As the old saying goes, you catch more flies with honey than with vinegar. And if that's true for filthy, ugly flies, it's also true of those mired in the filth of sin.

God doesn't need more prosecuting attorneys. He needs more witnesses who will tell the truth about Him.

God's purpose for ancient Israel might have succeeded, had they cooperated with Him. God could not have given His chosen people any more of what they needed to be His representatives. He held nothing back:

"God desired to make of His people Israel a praise and a glory. Every spiritual advantage was given them. God withheld from them nothing favorable to the formation of character that would make them representatives of Himself"—*COL*, p. 288.

But despite all of God's promised blessings—despite the unlimited resources He made available—Israel ultimately failed in carrying out God's plan. And because they refused to meet the conditions God had set, they largely missed out on His blessings.

Imagine what Israel might have enjoyed:

"If obedient, they would be preserved from the diseases that afflicted other nations, and would be blessed with vigor of intellect. The glory of God, His majesty and power, were to be revealed in all their prosperity. They were to be a kingdom of priests and princes. God furnished them with every facility for becoming the greatest nation on the earth"—*COL*, Ibid.

▸ Protection from disease.

▸ Intellectual vigor.

▸ Prosperity.

▶ Every imaginable blessing.

Israel might have been the marvel of the world—the greatest nation on earth. But tragically, they would spend long centuries in defeat and captivity.

Seven haunting, pointed words capture Israel's ultimate failure:

"But Israel did not fulfill God's purpose"—*COL*, p. 290.

How did this—how *could* this—happen?

"They forgot God, and lost sight of their high privilege as His representatives. The blessings they had received brought no blessing to the world. All their advantages were appropriated for their own glorification. They robbed God of the service He required of them, and they robbed their fellow men of religious guidance and a holy example"—*COL*, pp. 291, 292.

As a nation, Israel might have fulfilled a mission from God so grand it can barely be taken in. But their failure was catastrophic:

"The Jewish people cherished the idea that they were the favorites of heaven, and that they were always to be exalted as the church of God. They were the children of Abraham, they declared, and so firm did the foundation of their prosperity seem to them that they defied earth and heaven to dispossess them of their rights. But by lives of unfaithfulness they were preparing for the condemnation of heaven and for separation from God"—*COL*, p. 294.

But though the Jewish nation finally cut itself off from God, this world was not left without men and women who stayed true to God—who loved Him with all their hearts and served Him loyally, no matter what.

The chain of the faithful remained unbroken.

As Jesus arrived on this earth as a newborn, some few of

these faithful ones welcomed His birth with joy and recognition, even as the overwhelming majority of Israel either rejected Him or did not even recognize Him.

Through Christ's growing-up years and His three-and-a-half years of ministry, this world was never without those who would rather die than be disloyal to their Creator and Messiah.

The story of this book is the story of the faithful few—a story we are following from Adam to the end of time. It is a story that is far more than just abstract history. For it is a story that involves you—and me. As never before, this year, this month, this day—there are only two sides when it comes to God: those who are faithful and loyal to Him—and those who choose to go their own way.

It's a choice you must face again before another night of sleep. And again tomorrow when you rise to face another day.

In every age, God has ALWAYS had a people—faithful and loyal, the called and chosen—and He still has a special people today.

CHAPTER 5

LOOKING FOR THE WRONG KING

Imagine going to work in the morning, then returning home in the evening to find that your family doesn't recognize you—that to them, you're a total stranger.

Or imagine going to a family reunion, only to find that no one there has the faintest idea who you are.

Let's hope nothing like this ever happens to you. But it did happen to Jesus.

"He was in the world, and the world was made through Him, and *the world did not know Him*. He came to His own, and *His own did not receive Him*"—John 1:10, 11, emphasis added.

Another Bible version puts it this way:

"But although the world was made through him, *the world didn't recognize him when he came*. Even in his own land and among his own people, *he was not accepted*"—New Living Translation, emphasis added.

It was bad enough that "the world" didn't know Jesus when He came to this earth. After all, He was their Creator too, whether they acknowledged Him or not—and He came to provide salvation not just for "His own" but for "the world."

Yes, bad enough that the world didn't recognize Him. But unbelievably, even "His own" rejected Him!

Though God shared at least three hundred specific prophecies foretelling the arrival of Jesus, His people rejected Him.

Though the scriptures were clear about how, where, and when Jesus would arrive, His people rejected Him.

But not all of them.

Let us note it well again: From the beginning, God has had an unbroken line of faithful followers who know Him, who are loyal to Him, and who trust and love Him. And from the beginning, they have been in the minority. They are the "few" who find and travel the narrow way that leads upward to life. The great majority take the easy way and walk the broad way that leads downward to destruction.

Some might think that if—when the history of this world is finally over—only the few are saved and find eternal life, while the great majority are lost and ultimately destroyed, then Satan must win and God must lose.

It's true that when earthly time ends and eternity begins, of the billions who have lived on the earth, those saved will indeed be in the minority. But remember these three things:

1. The saving life and death of Jesus provided free salvation for everyone. He "is longsuffering toward us, not willing that *any* should perish but that *all* should come to repentance"—2 Peter 3:9, emphasis added. So God doesn't choose some to be saved and some to be lost. Each person—using the power of free choice God gave at Creation to every man and woman—ultimately decides his or her own destiny.

2. The end of the great controversy between good and evil—between Christ and Satan—isn't here yet. In the final, dramatic showdown before Jesus returns, a vast multitude will join Christ's faithful followers. Some will

cross over from the side of the enemy. Some who have tried to avoid making a choice will make one. We can't yet say that the minority who are ultimately saved will be a pathetically small number. After all, John the Revelator—previewing Heaven—saw *"a great multitude which no one could number,* of all nations, tribes, peoples, and tongues, standing before the throne and before the Lamb, clothed with white robes, with palm branches in their hands"—Revelation 7:9, emphasis added.

3.   Finally, the prophet Isaiah says that when the controversy is over, Jesus Himself "shall see the labor of His soul, and be satisfied"—Isaiah 53:11. The enormous sacrifice Jesus made to save men and women, He will consider well worth all that He gave, all the pain He endured, even to His death.

So we need not be concerned that the loyal followers of Jesus are—and have ever been—few in number. And when Jesus arrived on this earth in fulfillment of promise and prophecy, those who were truly His were so few that the Bible could accurately state that "His own"—the nation He had chosen to represent Him on earth—did not receive Him.

How could this be?

Unseeing Eyes, Unhearing Ears

They had the prophecies. God made sure that no detail about Christ's arrival was withheld from them. But long and repeated apostasy had blinded the eyes of God's chosen nation—especially its leaders. They had eyes with which to read, but could not see. They had ears with which they heard the prophets, but they could not hear.

Driven by the same spirit that impelled Lucifer to exalt himself, they were filled with an overpowering desire to become such a great nation that they could dominate and control all other nations. But the national greatness God had wanted for them was the greatness of servanthood, not the power of military dominance.

Yes, Israel believed in a coming Messiah, but they had imposed on the prophecies of His arrival their own preconceived desires. They didn't want—and weren't looking for—a Messiah who would come in poverty and humility, born in a stable of parents too poor to afford the cost of a room. No, they wanted a conquering King—a military leader who would deliver them from the oppression of the hated Romans.

They were looking for the wrong Messiah, so they missed His arrival.

But not everyone did.

Some Looked for the Right King

To humble shepherds in a field, an angel appeared and announced Christ's birth. Filled with awe, the shepherds traveled to see the newborn King. Wise Men from the East saw a magnificent star in the night sky and followed it to Christ's birthplace to worship Him.

And all through His life on this earth, a loyal few believed in Jesus and followed Him. His parents. John the Baptist and the many who responded to his preaching. Mary, Martha, and Lazarus. The twelve disciples. The countless honest-hearted in Israel who heard Jesus teach, saw His miracles, and opened themselves to the conviction of the Holy Spirit—these too took their place in the unbroken line of the faithful.

And when the life and ministry of Jesus reached the pinnacle of its purpose one dark Friday on a hideous cross, not everyone in the frenzied crowd called for His death. Simon the Cyrene carried the cross of Jesus, and his steps took him to the side of right and truth and salvation. A Roman soldier chose which side He would join. To one side of Jesus, a thief made the same decision—as did many in the clamoring crowd at the foot of the cross.

Who can really know but God Himself how many made their choice for Christ during His life on earth? Someday, we *will* know—and doubtless we'll be amazed when we find out.

When Jesus had completed what He had come to Earth to accomplish, the Bible says He ascended back to Heaven, to sit at the right hand of God the Father. But before He left this earth, He would begin a new and different kind of Israel. This time, instead of choosing a single nation, He would open this new and spiritual Israel to everyone, inviting every man, woman, and child to follow Him.

Jesus would establish His Church—and His followers would carry His name, being known as *Christians.* Through His Church, Jesus would ensure and extend the line of the faithful into the future. His Church would continue from His ascension to His second coming.

The Church began with miraculous success. Thousands were converted in a day. The truth and love of Jesus would spread over the earth like wildfire. But just as with Israel, the Church too would be opposed by Satan. It would be infiltrated by error. It would compromise with the world around it. It would slide into apostasy and idolatry and heresy, until again, only a faithful few could be found within its borders.

It can be sad—depressing even—to review the history of Israel and see how far short they fell of God's breathtaking purpose for them. It can be just as sobering to study the history of God's second Israel, His Church, and trace its repeated departures from His purpose for it.

But mark it well: At its darkest hour—at the depth of its apostasies—there were *always, always* the faithful few in Israel who had "not bowed the knee to Baal." And the history of the Church proves that at its most corrupt, there have *always, always* been the faithful few who have followed Jesus with a faith that cannot be shaken.

Let's return now to the birth of the Christian Church and

follow its journey through its earliest decades. And if we discover—as we will—that soon after its founding, the Church on the track of time derailed and careened into apostasy, then instead of lamenting that tragedy, let us discover and celebrate the faithful few who stood firmly on the side of right, come what may. For these are our spiritual ancestors. These are the strong links in the unbroken chain of which we too can aspire to be links.

As you read these words, the entire world population of 6.5 billion is lining up on one side of the great controversy or the other. By active choice or passive default, a tragic majority are choosing the wrong side. But God has His faithful, even at this very moment. They love Him fervently. They have a heart to obey Him. They choose to believe Him. They will stand for His truth and defend His character to their last breath.

Have you chosen—no looking back—which side you are on in this great controversy? If not, why wait—why not make this the day you do?

And if you have, this can be another day in which you let the world and the universe know exactly where you stand.

In every age, God has ALWAYS had a people—faithful and loyal, the called and chosen—and He still has a special people today.

CHAPTER 6

FIRESTORM!

As a young man, I worked summers in the forests of Oregon—in America's Pacific Northwest—on a logging operation. One uncomfortably hot and dry August afternoon, about fifty feet from where I stood, I saw a moving cable of wire rope strike against a rock, sending a bright spark into the tinder-dry grass of the forest floor. A flame instantly erupted, then spread rapidly in every direction.

Racing over, I tore off my tin hat and T-shirt and flailed at the flames in a vain effort to put them out. But the flames were already racing in a widening circle too large to contain.

Logging operations ceased as the entire crew did their best to fight back the fire, but the day was too hot, the grass too dry, the trees too parched. By evening, huge planes overhead dropped their loads of pink fire retardant on a fire that now had consumed several hundred acres. It would be days before the fire was fully controlled.

From that day forward, I could never think of Pentecost without remembering that fire in the Oregon mountains.

Jesus spent three years in ministry on this earth. He didn't try to evangelize His chosen people, Israel. He didn't try to evangelize the nonbelieving gentiles. Yes, by lakeside and mountainside, He told parables—simple stories that helped people understand His spiritual kingdom. But He held no evangelistic meetings, did not crisscross the map in a frenetic attempt to win the world, worked no miracles to reach everyone on earth with His message of love and grace.

Instead, Jesus poured Himself into twelve simple men who trusted Him enough to leave their livelihoods and follow Him—learn of Him—for a little over three years. They followed Him as He ministered to all who needed Him, as He healed the lame and the blind, as He told the truth about God, as He demonstrated what love looks like at close range.

He placed in each of those twelve hearts a spark. But these hearts were not yet dry and thirsty enough to erupt into sheets of flame. They were like green wood, not dry. As Christ's ministry reached its high point at the Cross, one of the twelve betrayed Him; another denied Him.

But all along, love burned quietly in the hearts of all but one. When after three days Jesus rose from the dead, the flames burned even brighter. Then He ascended out of the view of His chosen disciples. But before He did, He told them that He would send His Holy Spirit to be with them.

So it was that they gathered afterward in the Upper Room and spent ten days in prayer and purging their hearts of fire-retarding selfishness. They sought the promised Holy Spirit and waited....

Then suddenly. . . "there came a sound from heaven, as of a rushing mighty wind, and it filled the whole house where they were sitting. Then there appeared to them divided tongues, as of fire, and one sat upon each of them. And they were all filled with the Holy Spirit"—Acts 2:2-4.

Pentecost!

The fire that had burned steadily in them for more than three years merged with the tongues of fire "upon" them. And we all know what a "rushing mighty wind" does to fire. Christ's followers were aflame with the power and passion of pure love—consumed in a firestorm of zeal and urgency and un-stoppable determination to win back the world to their risen Lord and Saviour. As they came down from the Upper Room, Peter spoke for them all, preaching with such Spirit-driven power that when he finished, three thousand people accepted Jesus and were baptized.

The Christian Church was born. And its momentum swept through the world so swiftly and relentlessly that before long, some who opposed the believers would complain of them as "those who have turned the world upside down"—Acts 17:6.

It seemed that the Christian Church—Christ's new Isra-el—was destined to quickly draw the entire world back to Christ with the powerful magnetism of His love and truth. Because the love of Christ—as demonstrated in His self-less life and His sacrificial death—had the power to do what nothing else could. It melted hearts. It destroyed self-will and made pride seem repulsive. And the truth of Christ—as He had taught and lived it—exposed Satan's lies for what they were and lifted up a Father-God determined to win back His rebel children.

Steady, Blue Flame

Mind you, the fire of Pentecost was no uncontrolled emo-tionalism, like the long, gaudy, billowing yellow flame of a newly lighted blowtorch. No, it was like a blowtorch that has been carefully adjusted so that its flame burns with a steady, fo-cused blue-white intensity. That white-hot flame of Pentecost was the result of God coming to completely fill willing human beings with Himself. And since God is love, each believer be-came a torch of love to set another afire. And each new torch set yet others afire, setting off a chain reaction moving from home to home, town to town, province to province.

And mind you also that the fire of God's love is not the same as the love so commonly celebrated in song and poetry and drama on this earth.

God's love doesn't give to get.

It isn't a rush of emotion.

It isn't quick infatuation.

It never quits when the going gets tough—when "the thrill is gone."

The love of God was most clearly seen at the Cross: utter and total self-sacrifice, not for people who deserved it, but for people who *needed* it. God loved those He created despite their rebellion—despite their desire to annihilate Him. He loved them because He had *made* them. They were His—and He would give His own life to save them.

Under Attack

At the cross, Satan's ultimate doom was sealed. It was now irreversible: he would lose the great controversy between himself and Christ. If he had aspired to be another superpower in the universe, his effort was now crippled. He was now a mortally wounded opponent—a lame-duck enemy.

But as long as he had life and breath, he would oppose Christ and His people—the Church. He would unleash the full force of selfishness and lies and do his level best to destroy this thriving but fledgling Church.

For those with eyes to see and ears to hear, Satan's counter-attacks would come as no surprise. As the Apostle Paul carried forward his ministry, first to converted Jews and then also to the gentiles, He issued this warning: "For I know this, that after my departure savage wolves will come in among you, not sparing the flock. Also from among yourselves men will rise up, speaking perverse things, to draw away the disciples after themselves. Therefore watch, and remember that for three years I did not cease to warn everyone night and day with tears"—Acts 20:29-31.

Satan would attack the young Church from outside—and from inside. From outside, savage wolves would come in to attack the flock. From inside, men would rise up speaking "perverse things."

Perverse things?

Paul elaborated in another church letter: "For the time will come when they will not endure sound doctrine, but according to their own desires, because they have itching ears, they will heap up for themselves teachers; and they will turn their ears away from the truth, and be turned aside to fables."—2 Timothy 4:3, 4.

Sound doctrine versus fables.

Truth versus lies.

The struggle between truth and lies—between sound doctrine and false doctrine—became so pronounced in one church that Paul was moved to rebuke it in the strongest possible words: "I marvel," Paul wrote, "that you are turning away so soon from Him who called you in the grace of Christ, to a different gospel, which is not another; but there are some who trouble you and want to pervert the gospel of Christ. But even if we, or an angel from heaven, preach any other gospel to you than what we have preached to you, let him be accursed. As we have said before, so now I say again, if anyone preaches any other gospel to you than what you have received, let him be accursed"—Galatians 1:6-9.

Paul reinforced his warnings against heresies rising up from within the Church by stating what few others had eyes to see. "The mystery of lawlessness," he said, "is already at work"—2 Thessalonians 2:7.

So even after the Cross, Satan kept up his war against Christ. He would yield nothing. He would attack God's character, His law, His truth, His gospel, His Church, and His people.

From Adam to Noah, Noah to Abraham, Abraham to Christ,

always, *always*—there were those who were faithful to God and His truth. Sometimes they were many, and sometimes (as with Noah at the time of the Flood) very few—as few as eight on the entire earth. But whether eight at the Flood or three thousand and more at Pentecost, the unbroken chain of the faithful has continued through time.

Who knows how many true believers followed Christ at the height of the early Church's success? Perhaps millions? What we do know is that just as Paul had forewarned, the great enemy would rouse himself to mount a full frontal attack on God's chosen ones. He would use both persecution from outside and heresy and compromise from inside to do his worst.

The entire history of the Christian Church—from Pentecost to the second coming of Jesus—is laid out in the book of Revelation. Its first three chapters contain messages to seven churches. The seven churches are really one continuous church—but at different times of history. The exact starting and ending dates for each church may not be precisely fixed—they vary even from one Bible scholar to another. But in general, here are the seven churches and their approximate time periods in history:

Ephesus	Pentecost to about A.D. 100
Smyrna	A.D. 100 to about A.D. 313
Pergamos	A.D. 313 to about A.D. 538
Thyatira	A.D. 538 to about A.D. 1517
Sardis	A.D. 1517 to about A.D. 1798
Philadelphia	A.D. 1798 to about A.D. 1844
Laodicea	A.D. 1844 to the end of time

In the remaining chapters of this book, we will follow the history of God's people in each of these time periods—under the symbols of these seven churches. Our next chapter will focus on the first three of these seven churches: Ephesus, Smyrna, and Pergamos.

From there, we will follow the Church through the long tunnel of the Dark Ages, under the symbol of Thyatira. The Church of the Reformation follows, under the symbol of Sardis. From the Reformation to the year 1844, we explore the church as it enters what history knows as the "great Advent awakening"—the church of Philadelphia.

With the year 1844, we reach the rise of the remnant—and the final chapters of this book will focus on the role of that remnant. These chapters should be of greatest interest and importance to you and me—because they are about US! They are about our privilege and obligation to continue in the unbroken line of the faithful. They are about how God wants to use us in our daily lives to win back His rebels. They are about knowing who we are and why we are here!

There's a line from Adam to you—and to me. In between, for some six thousand years or more, God has forged His unbroken chain of the faithful and loyal.

I want to be a strong link in that chain—a link to which others can in turn link up to extend the chain through time a little longer, till the great battle finally ends.

And it will end, my friend.

Soon—but not yet.

> *In every age, God has ALWAYS had a people—faithful and loyal, the called and chosen—and He still has a special people today.*

CHAPTER 7

BRING ON THE RAIN

Whether he actually set the fire, history can't say for certain. But history does confirm that he took the early blame for it.

Until, that is, he found a scapegoat.

When a firestorm swept the city of Rome in A.D. 64, leaving only four of its fourteen districts intact, rumors swept the citizenry that the emperor himself—Nero (who ruled from A.D. 54 – 68)—had set the fire. Rumors also circulated that during the week the flames continued, Nero played his lyre and sang from a hilltop as the city burned. Over the years, this turned into the legend that Nero fiddled as Rome burned—not likely, as the fiddle had not yet been invented.

To deflect the unwelcome suspicions of the populace, Nero accused the Christians living in the city. In the words of the Roman historian Tacitus:

> "And so, to get rid of this rumor, Nero set up as the culprits and punished with the utmost refinement of cruelty a class hated for their abominations, who are commonly called Christians. Nero's scapegoats were the perfect choice because it temporarily relieved pressure of the various rumors going around Rome."

Their abominations?

Why the ill will against these early Christians?

Just as false allegations had led to the death of Jesus Christ—the founder of the Church—just so, similar lies would spread concerning His followers. In the great controversy between good and evil, between Christ and Satan, Jesus had won the decisive battle at the Cross of Calvary. Satan's ultimate doom was sealed when Jesus cried out, "It is finished!"

But though Satan's ultimate fate was settled that dark Friday, other issues in the contest between Heaven's once-highest angel and His Creator remained to be resolved. Questions about God's fairness, about His Law, His government, and His character remained to be fully answered.

Once Jesus returned to His Father's side in Heaven, Satan focused his insatiable fury on Christ's followers on earth. While Jesus walked the roads of Palestine, Satan stirred up all kinds of horrible lies against Him. Now he continued the same tactic against Christ's followers.

Rumors spread like the flames of Rome. The practice of the Lord's Supper led to wild allegations of human sacrifice and cannibalism. The Sabbath rest led to charges of laziness. Christians were said to engage in wild orgies and other depraved behaviors.

So when Nero diverted suspicion for the great fire from himself to the Christians, it was an easy sell. Historians of the era record that the persecution that followed was fueled not so much by blame for the fire as by the prevailing view that Christians were enemies of humanity.

And the persecution was horrific.

Tacitus again: "Covered with the skins of beasts, they were torn by dogs and perished, or were nailed to crosses, or were doomed to the flames and burnt, to serve as a nightly illumination, when daylight had expired."

Christians, burned alive as torches to illuminate the night sky. Crucified. Mauled to death by dogs. Yes, horrific.

"The powers of earth and hell," wrote Ellen White, "arrayed themselves against Christ in the person of His followers. Paganism foresaw that should the gospel triumph, her temples and altars would be swept away; therefore she summoned her forces to destroy Christianity"—*The Great Controversy*, p. 39.

"From Olivet the Saviour beheld the storms about to fall upon the apostolic church; and penetrating deeper into the future, His eye discerned the fierce, wasting tempests that were to beat upon His followers in the coming ages of darkness and persecution"—Ibid.

There on Olivet, Jesus uttered these words: "Then they will deliver you up to tribulation and kill you, and you will be hated by all nations for My name's sake"—Matthew 24:9.

The persecution of those early faithful Christians did not end with Nero but continued for centuries. History records at least ten major persecutions of Christians that began under Nero and continued under his successors:

▶ Nero (A.D. 64)
▶ Domitian (c. 90–96)
▶ Trajan (98–117)
▶ Hadrian (117–138)
▶ Marcus Aurelius (161–181)
▶ Septimus Severus (202–211)
▶ Maximus the Thracian (235–251)
▶ Decius (249–251)
▶ Valerian (257–260)
▶ Diocletian / Galerius (303–311)

"These persecutions, beginning under Nero about the time of the martyrdom of Paul, continued with greater or less fury for centuries. Christians were falsely accused of the most dreadful crimes and declared to be the cause of great calamities—famine, pestilence, and earthquake. As they became the objects of popular hatred and suspicion, informers stood ready, for the sake of gain, to betray the innocent. They were condemned as rebels against the empire, as foes of religion, and pests to society. Great numbers were thrown to wild beasts or burned alive in the amphitheaters. Some were crucified; others were covered with the skins of wild animals and thrust into the arena to be torn by dogs. Their punishment was often made the chief entertainment at public fetes. Vast multitudes assembled to enjoy the sight and greeted their dying agonies with laughter and applause"—*The Great Controversy*, p. 40.

Of these faithful, the Bible says: "Still others had trial of mockings and scourgings, yes, and of chains and imprisonment. They were stoned, they were sawn in two, were tempted, were slain with the sword. They wandered about in sheepskins and goatskins, being destitute, afflicted, tormented—of whom the world was not worthy. They wandered in deserts and mountains, in dens and caves of the earth"—Hebrews 11:36-38.

The result of this unrelenting persecution? Did it succeed in discouraging those early Christians? Did the horror of it all prove too much? Were they so dispirited that finally, they gave up?

"In vain were Satan's efforts to destroy the church of Christ by violence. . . . By defeat they conquered"—*The Great Controversy*, p. 41.

"The Blood of Christians Is Seed"

As Tertullian wrote: "The oftener we are mown down by you, the more in number we grow; the blood of Christians is seed."

What Satan was attempting wasn't working. And grant the

great enemy this: he is no dimwit. The towering intelligence with which he'd been blessed at his creation did not vanish when he fell through pride. He simply refocused his bright mind toward evil.

Clearly, it was time for a complete change of strategy.

"The great adversary now endeavored to gain by artifice what he had failed to secure by force. Persecution ceased, and in its stead were substituted the dangerous allurements of temporal prosperity and worldly honor. Idolaters were led to receive a part of the Christian faith, while they rejected other essential truths. They professed to accept Jesus as the Son of God and to believe in His death and resurrection, but they had no conviction of sin and felt no need of repentance or of a change of heart. With some concessions on their part they proposed that Christians should make concessions, that all might unite on the platform of belief in Christ.

"Now the church was in fearful peril. Prison, torture, fire, and sword were blessings in comparison with this. Some of the Christians stood firm, declaring that they could make no compromise. Others were in favor of yielding or modifying some features of their faith and uniting with those who had accepted a part of Christianity, urging that this might be the means of their full conversion. That was a time of deep anguish to the faithful followers of Christ. Under a cloak of pretended Christianity, Satan was insinuating himself into the church, to corrupt their faith and turn their minds from the word of truth.

"Most of the Christians at last consented to lower their standard, and a union was formed between Christianity and paganism"—*The Great Controversy*, pp. 42, 43.

Persecution hadn't worked. But compromise? Here, the enemy largely succeeded.

Under the symbols of seven churches, the book of Revelation traces the entire history of the Christian Church from its founding to the return of its Founder. And though, as noted in the previous chapter, the exact starting and ending dates for each church vary from one Bible scholar to another, the approximate time periods for the first three churches are as follows:

Ephesus	Pentecost to about A.D. 100
Smyrna	A.D. 100 to about A.D. 313
Pergamos	A.D. 313 to about A.D. 538

Ephesus

Notice now the message God sends to Ephesus, the first of the seven:

> "To the angel of the church of Ephesus write, 'These things says He who holds the seven stars in His right hand, who walks in the midst of the seven golden lampstands: "I know your works, your labor, your patience, and that you cannot bear those who are evil. And you have tested those who say they are apostles and are not, and have found them liars; and you have persevered and have patience, and have labored for My name's sake and have not become weary. Nevertheless I have this against you, that you have left your first love. Remember therefore from where you have fallen; repent and do the first works, or else I will come to you quickly and remove your lampstand from its place—unless you repent"'"—Revelation 2:1-5.

It is outside the scope of the story we're telling in this book to explain in detail every word and phrase of these messages to the seven churches. But note this much about this first message: God acknowledges the "works" and "patience" of these earliest Christians.

Driven by a love for their Leader stronger than death itself, these first Christians endured the most horrific persecutions imaginable. They were faithful and loyal, no matter what the price.

But in time, some began to waver. Some began to lose their connection with their Leader. Some began to take their relationship with Jesus for granted.

It happens all too often. Newlyweds, in the consuming fire of first love, would do anything for each other—even die, if that were necessary. But time and stress and carelessness can bring a change so slow it's not even noticed. The fire of first love dies down and can yield to glowing embers—or even cold coals and ashes.

Perhaps it's unrealistic for the passion and intensity of first love to continue indefinitely. In good marriages, it eventually transforms into something more sustainable—a steady, deep mutual appreciation and commitment and bonding that is stronger, richer, and more lasting than even the romantic fires of "first love."

But sadly, "first love" all too often gives way to boredom and irritation and apathy, leaving only the dead coals of what once was.

To the Church of Ephesus, God said: "You have left your first love. Repent—and do the first works." Many troubled relationships can be saved when the partners begin to do again for each other those things they once did so effortlessly.

Though by roughly the year A.D. 100—the endpoint of the Ephesus Church time period—persecution had already begun, the Head of the Church found it necessary to warn that while some remained steadfast even to death, others were allowing complacency to replace their passionate first love.

The Head of the Church knew that His followers could not endure if they carelessly allowed this to happen. Repent, return, reclaim your original zeal, He urged them. They would desperately need that first love, for Smyrna was just around the corner.

Smyrna

Smyrna—the Church from about A.D. 100 to 313—would be the Church during its period of most intense persecution. God's letter to Smyrna is the only one of the seven that contains no rebuke.

> "And to the angel of the church in Smyrna write, 'These things says the First and the Last, who was dead, and came to life: "I know your works, tribulation, and poverty (but you are rich); and I know the blasphemy of those who say they are Jews and are not, but are a synagogue of Satan. Do not fear any of those things which you are about to suffer. Indeed, the devil is about to throw some of you into prison, that you may be tested, and you will have tribulation ten days. Be faithful until death, and I will give you the crown of life"'"—Revelation 2:9, 10.

For those who would face death for their faith, it must certainly have been comforting and encouraging to be reminded that their Lord "was dead, and came to life." Just so would they.

I know, said their Leader, what you are about to face. I know that some of you will be imprisoned for your faithfulness. Some of you will die. But do not be afraid. If you are faithful even to death, I will give you a crown of life.

What Jesus said to the Church of Smyrna holds true for the Church at the very end of time. Just before the Second Coming of Christ, some of His followers will once again face death for their faith. Possibly that could include some of us now living. The promise of a crown of life is for those at the end as well.

"You will have tribulation for ten days," God says. And while it is true that persecutions continued intermittently all through the early centuries under various Roman emperors, it is widely acknowledged that the most bloody and intense of them took place over a ten-year period, from A.D. 303–313, under the emperor Diocletian. Applying the year-for-a-day principle of interpreting Bible prophecy (see Numbers 14:34; Ezekiel 4:6), ten days would equal ten years.

Pergamos

We arrive now at the Church that represents Satan's shift in strategy from persecution to compromise. From A.D. 313 to 538, paganism and Christianity grew ever more intertwined. And during this time, the Roman Church came to dominate Christianity, ushering in a host of practices and doctrines unknown to the early Church. Finally, the line separating the Church and "state" (government) grew increasingly blurred.

"And to the angel of the church in Pergamos write, 'These things says He who has the sharp two-edged sword: "I know your works, and where you dwell, where Satan's throne is. And you hold fast to My name, and did not deny My faith even in the days in which Antipas was My faithful martyr, who was killed among you, where Satan dwells. But I have a few things against you, because you have there those who hold the doctrine of Balaam, who taught Balak to put a stumbling block before the children of Israel, to eat things sacrificed to idols, and to commit sexual immorality. Thus you also have those who hold the doctrine of the Nicolaitans, which thing I hate. Repent, or else I will come to you quickly and will fight against them with the sword of My mouth"'"—Revelation 2:12-15.

Again, without attempting to address all the detail in this message, it is clear that Jesus reminds His people of their faithfulness even to martyrdom, but calls them to account for compromising the purity of their doctrines. They had accepted error in place of truth.

From the supposed "conversion" of the emperor Constantine in A.D. 313, when he made Christianity the state religion, to the establishment of full papal power in 538, Christianity steadily compromised. The Bible seventh-day Sabbath gave way to a counterfeit Sunday Sabbath. The Bible as the one true authority for Christians yielded its place to human tradition. Religious freedom came to be termed heresy. Salvation was no longer a free gift but a reward for unaided human effort.

We've noted that when Satan saw that persecution was not working to destroy Christ's followers, he shifted to the tactic of compromise. But does that suggest that Satan has forever abandoned persecution?

Quite evidently, no.

"There is another and more important question that should engage the attention of the churches of today. The apostle Paul declares that 'all that will live godly in Christ Jesus shall suffer persecution.' 2 Timothy 3:12. Why is it, then, that persecution seems in a great degree to slumber? The only reason is that the church has conformed to the world's standard and therefore awakens no opposition. The religion which is current in our day is not of the pure and holy character that marked the Christian faith in the days of Christ and His apostles. It is only because of the spirit of compromise with sin, because the great truths of the word of God are so indifferently regarded, because there is so little vital godliness in the church, that Christianity is apparently so popular with the world. Let there be a revival of the faith and power of the early church, and the spirit of persecution will be revived, and the fires of persecution will be rekindled"—*The Great Controversy*, p. 48.

If Satan's efforts in those early centuries to entice Christians into compromise had *NOT* succeeded—had they remained steadfastly loyal—the implication in the comment above is that Satan would have returned to persecuting, perhaps intensifying it.

Why no persecution today of the kind the early Christians endured? Because compromise continues all too well to succeed—not just on a Church level (indifference concerning Bible truths) but personally (compromise with sin).

Any Adventist knows, though, that a Latter Rain is coming. We know that a great revival will happen before the very end. We know that "primitive godliness" will once again prevail.

And when that happens, persecution will return. A time of trouble will begin. All that the early Christians endured—and more—God's people at the end will experience.

To some, this is frightening. Any one of us may wonder if we have the strength to stand firm for truth and for the one who is Truth, even through persecution and death. Could we endure torture? Starvation? Imprisonment? Death?

Grace When It's Needed

"My grace," God says, "is sufficient for you, for My strength is made perfect in weakness."—2 Corinthians 12:9.

Today—this moment—you may not have grace for persecution, for death. Because today, that is not what you face. But if a time comes that God asks, allows, yes, even honors you as one to face these things, then and *ONLY* then, He will give you the grace for that moment.

Yet, how faithful I am to my Lord today is a preparation for how faithful I would be then. How loyal I am—how faithful you are—today to God's truth is a measure of how faithful we'd be then.

Through Ephesus, Smyrna, and Pergamos, God always had His faithful and loyal ones. They stood in that unbroken line that began with Adam and will continue through all time here on earth. It's an unbroken chain of which you and I are links.

When the time of greatest trial comes, we want to stand firm. Our best preparation? To forge the strongest possible connection to the Source of strength. Today—tomorrow—and every day.

One of country singer Jo Dee Messina's hits that climbed the charts contained these words: "Tomorrow's another day... and I'm thirsty anyway...so bring on the rain."

Is there an Adventist anywhere who can't echo that sentiment and apply it to our hopes of a coming revival?

Yes, tomorrow's another day. And I'm ever so thirsty, Lord.

So bring on the rain—the Latter Rain.

In every age, God has ALWAYS had a people—faithful and loyal, the called and chosen—and He still has a special people today.

CHAPTER 8

WILDERNESS WOMAN

Hollywood's movie industry is like a surfer—always looking for the next big wave.

If it notices that religiously themed books are topping the best seller lists, it rushes to cash in. When the *Left Behind* book series set publishing records around the world, it paved the way for American actor Mel Gibson to produce *The Passion of the Christ*. And when that movie did well at the box office, other producers lost no time in coming out with *The Da Vinci Code* and *The Lion, the Witch, and the Wardrobe*.

Never mind that Hollywood never seems to get it right. If not deliberately appealing to emotionalism, they peddle a "religion" that is frankly erroneous or anti-biblical—or that employs the vehicle of fantasy.

If the moviemakers really want a religious movie to dazzle viewers—something with gripping drama that would challenge their special effects—they should bring the prophecies of the Bible's books of Daniel and Revelation to the big screen. But just as well they don't, since they would try to "improve" on the story by changing it. They can't leave well enough alone.

But you can't improve on the stories of Daniel and the

Revelation. Take, for example, the story of the Dragon and the Woman.

As an Adventist, you undoubtedly know the story well. If so, then you already *know* it's a good one! So switch on that widescreen, high-definition, giant screen in your imagination, and see again the drama of Revelation 12:

> "Now a great sign appeared in heaven: a woman clothed with the sun, with the moon under her feet, and on her head a garland of twelve stars. Then being with child, she cried out in labor and in pain to give birth. And another sign appeared in heaven: behold, a great, fiery red dragon having seven heads and ten horns, and seven diadems on his heads. His tail drew a third of the stars of heaven and threw them to the earth. And the dragon stood before the woman who was ready to give birth, to devour her Child as soon as it was born."—Revelation 12:1-4.

Good story writers use a technique called a "flashback," in which they interrupt the story they're telling to reach back to an earlier point in time. The apostle John—the author of Revelation—was a good writer. In the verses above, John said that with his tail, the dragon "drew a third of the stars of heaven and threw them to the earth."

The story moves on, but later, John flashes back to the time when the "stars of heaven" were thrown to the earth.

> "And war broke out in heaven: Michael and his angels fought with the dragon; and the dragon and his angels fought, but they did not prevail, nor was a place found for them in heaven any longer. So the great dragon was cast out, that serpent of old, called the Devil and Satan, who deceives the whole world; he was cast to the earth, and his angels were cast out with him"—Revelation 12:7-9.

The dragon's angels—"a third of the stars of heaven"—were cast out of Heaven with him.

These three verses briefly describe the very beginning of the great controversy between good and evil. When the dragon (clearly identified here as the Devil, or Satan—the fallen angel Lucifer) declared war on God, he and the one-third of Heaven's angels he had deceived with his lies fought against Michael (Christ).

Woman in the Wilderness

But on earth, Satan the dragon continued his war against God. A careful study of Revelation makes clear that a woman is a symbol of a church. Here in Revelation 12 we see a good woman. In Revelation 17, you can find a very bad woman.

Here in our story, the woman is ready to give birth, and John paints for us a picture of a snarling dragon waiting to pounce on her child the instant it is born. But God protected the woman and her child.

"She bore a male Child who was to rule all nations with a rod of iron. And her Child was caught up to God and His throne. Then the woman fled into the wilderness, where she has a place prepared by God, that they should feed her there one thousand two hundred and sixty days" Revelation 12:5, 6.

This male Child was none other than Jesus Himself—the same Michael against whom the dragon had fought in Heaven. Now Jesus had come to earth to be born as a baby, grow to manhood, and become the Savior of the human race.

But after His life, death, and resurrection, Jesus was "caught up to God and His throne." The dragon then turned his full attention on the woman—the Church Jesus established before He ascended to Heaven.

John says she "fled into the wilderness," where God fed her there for "one thousand two hundred and sixty days."

"Now when the dragon saw that he had been cast to the

earth, he persecuted the woman who gave birth to the male Child. But the woman was given two wings of a great eagle, that she might fly into the wilderness to her place, where she is nourished for a time and times and half a time, from the presence of the serpent"—Revelation 12:13, 14.

A time and times and half a time. One thousand two hundred and sixty days. What is this?

In time prophecies, the Bible says a day equals a year (see Numbers 14:34; Ezekiel 4:6). In prophetic reckoning, a year also contains 360 days. So let's do a little math. One thousand two hundred and sixty days (1,260) would equal 1,260 years. Comparing Bible verses, it becomes evident that a "time" also equals a year. So a "time" (360 days) plus "times" (2 x 360 days, or 720 days) plus "half a time" (180 days) adds up to 1,260 days—are we right, math majors?

The "one thousand two hundred and sixty days" of verse 6 are the same as the "time and times and half a time" of verse 14.

The woman would be in the wilderness for 1,260 years.

Now let's make things more interesting. Notice this in the Old Testament book of Daniel:

"He shall speak pompous words against the Most High, shall persecute the saints of the Most High, and shall intend to change times and law. Then the saints shall be given into his hand for a time and times and half a time"—Daniel 7:25.

The "he" here is a great and fearsome ten-horned beast. But notice how long this great power would "persecute the saints": "a time and times and half a time." Sound familiar?

Both Daniel and Revelation predict a period of 1,260 years. Daniel said that during this time, the saints would be persecuted. Revelation says that during this time, the woman would be persecuted. The woman. The Church. The saints. All one and the same.

Keeping an eye on both Daniel and Revelation, we notice several things that happen during this period of 1,260 years.

▶ The saints are persecuted (or, the woman).

▶ The woman flees into the wilderness, to a place God has prepared, where she is fed and nourished.

▶ A great power rules that "speaks pompous words against the Most High."

▶ This power persecutes the saints.

▶ And this power intends to "change times and laws."

Most Seventh-day Adventist Bible students already know the details of the 1,260-year prophecy. If this includes you, then you know that this great beastly power that ruled was a union of apostolic Christianity with paganism that led to the rise of the papal power.

Growing Power of the Bishop at Rome

The "bishops" or leaders of early Christian churches at first had no central governing authority. But in time, the church in one area grew stronger—and its bishop more prominent: the church at Rome. Other bishops began to look for guidance to the practices of the church there—or sought the direction of its bishop.

When—as we noticed in the previous chapter—paganism marched into the Church, nowhere was this more successful than in the Church of the emperor's home city. In the early fourth century under the emperor Constantine, Christianity became the state religion—or at least of a "kind of" Christianity. For by now, a compromising Church had welcomed a host of pagan doctrines and practices that bore no resemblance to the Christianity of the earliest Christians.

The authority and power of the bishop—or *papa* (pope)—at Rome steadily grew, so that he could issue edicts binding on other Christian churches. Then, in the year A.D. 533, the

Roman emperor Justinian issued a decree to set up the bishop of Rome as the "head of all the Holy Churches." But certain other powers in the Roman Empire had to be driven out before this decree could take effect. Those powers were defeated in the year 538, and from that time forward—for the next 1,260 years—the power of the papacy was supreme.

Both this current chapter—and the next—will focus on this 1,260-year period. If you've been reading right along, you know we've been following in order the seven churches of Revelation. The 1,260 years includes two of them: Thyatira, from A.D. 538 to 1517—and Sardis, from A.D. 1517 to 1798. So for now, we're focusing on the time frame of Thyatira. Chapter 9 will turn to Sardis.

Sadly, by A.D. 538, the Roman church had become a system riddled with false teachings and practices. Human tradition and papal edict became more authoritative than the Bible. The Bible was locked away from all but the priests. Access to God was only through the priesthood. Salvation was through a system of religious works. Purgatory, indulgences, Mariolatry, baptism by sprinkling, Peter as the founder of the Church, papal infallibility, the mass, transubstantiation, confession of sin to the priests, worship of images—the errors multiplied. All unbiblical. All utterly unknown to the first Christians.

But if all this falsehood was sad, then sadder still was the determination of the Roman church to impose its teachings, its practices, and its will by force. Those who would not yield were persecuted and many were ultimately destroyed.

But all through these Dark Ages from A.D. 538 to the breaking of papal power in 1798, God had a faithful people—humble but determined believers who were loyal to their Lord even if it meant persecution. Even if it meant torture and death.

They would stay true to God's truth, no matter what. They would continue to worship on His seventh-day Sabbath—not the man-made Sunday Sabbath enforced by the Roman church.

They would continue to hold the Bible—and the Bible only—as their authority—not the traditions and edicts of fallible men. They would stay true to the Bible truth about salvation, baptism, or the state of the dead.

Under siege, these loyal ones fled to "the wilderness." These believers—the Church, the woman—looked for a refuge in the mountains and unpopulated areas. Notice Satan's pursuit:

> "So the serpent spewed water out of his mouth like a flood after the woman, that he might cause her to be carried away by the flood. But the earth helped the woman, and the earth opened its mouth and swallowed up the flood which the dragon had spewed out of his mouth"—Revelation 12:15, 16.

Earth and Water

Water? In Bible prophecy, water is a symbol of people—of densely populated areas (see Revelation 17:15). The serpent, the dragon, sent "a flood" of water after the woman. A flood of *people.* And the only kind of people that could come out of the mouth of the evil dragon are very bad people!

But "the earth" swallowed up this flood of persecuting, pursuing evil people. If water is a symbol of many people, then by contrast, the "earth" is a symbol of a relatively unpopulated area.

Not only did God's true followers find shelter, during the worst of the persecutions, in remote mountain areas, but before the end of the 1,260 years, countless millions would flee religious oppression to find their way to a very sparsely populated New World.

As the 1,260 years began, the Roman church, with its newly granted monopoly on power, began aggressively to enforce its beliefs and practices, seeking to bring the entire world under its dominion. To do this, it resorted to persecution that persisted for centuries.

But the unbroken chain of the faithful and loyal remained unbroken through it all. Through all the dark centuries, some never abandoned God or His truth. They never compromised. They never denied their faith in order to save themselves.

Among these, consider the true stories of the Albigenses and the Waldenses. A woman in the wilderness? Never more true than with these believers, who fled to the highest mountains of Europe to escape the persecution of the Roman church. In the chapter to follow, the story of another band of the faithful—the Huguenots, who stood unwaveringly for truth in the time of the Reformation—will be recounted.

The Albigenses

In the early 12th century, a group of reform-minded Christians separated from the Roman Catholic Church—no longer able conscientiously to accept or believe in the many nonbiblical doctrines of the Church.

Known as the Albigenses (after the town of Albi in Southern France—about twenty-two miles north of present-day Toulouse), these believers preached against such Catholic teachings as the human priesthood, worship of saints and idols, and the elevation of papal authority above that of the Bible. By A.D. 1167, the Albigenses comprised the majority of the population of Southern France.

Did the Albigenses teach and believe every truth of today's Seventh-day Adventist Church? No. Did they even have some beliefs we today could not accept? Yes. But they loved their Lord and chose death rather than disloyalty to Him.

Considering the Albigenses a threat to their power and control, the Catholic Church reacted with force. In 1208, the ironically named Pope Innocent III ordered a crusade of extermination against the falsely labeled "heretics." The papal armies marched through Albigensian territory, and whole towns were massacred. The systematic slaughter of these believers continued for decades, in time intensifying as the Church ordered a series of papal inquisitions—even more aggressive campaigns of torture and murder to exterminate the so-called heretics.

The papal campaign was successful. Within a hundred years of their beginnings, the Albigensians were utterly exterminated. To the last believer, they remained faithful to their understanding of the Word of God—and immovable in their opposition to papal false doctrine and pagan Church practices.

The Waldenses

In the early A.D. 1170s, Peter Waldo, a wealthy merchant of Lyons, France, organized a band of believers that at first came to be known as the Poor Men of Lyons—lay members of the Catholic Church who followed their leader in giving away their property, believing that apostolic poverty was the path of Christian growth.

In 1179, they went to Rome, where Pope Alexander III blessed them but forbade them to preach unless authorized by the local clergy. But the Waldenses (or Vaudois, as they were also known in the French language), disobeyed Rome and began to teach the truths they had discovered in the Bible.

They proclaimed the Bible as their sole rule of faith and life practice. And they preached against such Catholic doctrines as purgatory, the papacy, the mass, and indulgences.

In 1184, they were formally declared heretics by Pope Lucius III—and this was confirmed later in the Fourth Lateran Council in 1215. But already, in 1211, more than eighty Waldenses were burned as heretics at Strasbourg—the beginning of several centuries of persecution.

Large numbers of Waldenses settled in Dauphiné and the Piedmont area—as well as in the Alps to the southwest of Turin.

In 1487, Pope Innocent VIII launched a brutal persecution to destroy the Waldenses. The Dauphiné Waldenses were over-whelmed, but the Piedmont believers successfully defended themselves.

Both the Church and the government of France continued the persecution of the Waldenses, many of whom fled into the Swiss Alps. Finally, in 1848, King Charles Albert of Savoy granted the Waldenses full civil and religious freedom. Soon after, a contingent of Waldenses emigrated to North Carolina in the United States.

"Among the leading causes that had led to the separation of the true church from Rome," wrote Ellen White, "was the hatred of the latter toward the Bible Sabbath. As foretold by prophecy, the papal power cast down the truth to the ground. The law of God was trampled in the dust, while the traditions and customs of men were exalted. . . . Through ages of darkness and apostasy there were Waldenses who denied the supremacy of Rome, who rejected image worship as idolatry, and who kept the true Sabbath. Under the fiercest tempests of opposition they maintained their faith."—*The Great Controversy*, p. 65.

> "Behind the lofty bulwarks of the mountains—in all ages the refuge of the persecuted and oppressed—the Waldenses found a hiding place. Here the light of truth was kept burning amid the darkness of the Middle Ages. Here, for a thousand years, witnesses for the truth maintained the ancient faith."—Ibid., pp. 65, 66.

The total number of Waldenses who died for their faith may never be known. Some sources conservatively estimate that 900,000 were put to death between the years of 1540 and 1570 alone.

> "The persecutions visited for many centuries upon this God-fearing people were endured by them with a patience and constancy that honored their Redeemer. Notwithstanding the crusades against them, and the inhuman butchery to which they were subjected, they continued to send out their

missionaries to scatter the precious truth. They were hunted to death; yet their blood watered the seed sown, and it failed not of yielding fruit."—*The Great Controversy,* p. 78.

For a more detailed history of the Waldenses, consider a thoughtful reading of Chapter 4 of *The Great Controversy.* No more inspiring source exists to reinforce the determination to stand for truth, come what may.

The Woman entered the Wilderness for 1,260 long, dark years—centuries of the most terrible persecution ever visited on God's faithful.

Friends, how many of us have a love for Jesus Christ and His truth that is too strong to be broken by persecution, by torture, by death? How many of us are prepared to stay loyal to our Saviour, no matter what?

On this earth—in this life—it often happens that a man and a woman fall in love. So deeply in love that either would without hesitation give his or her life for the other, should that ever be necessary. Are we cultivating the kind of relationship with Jesus each day that fuels a love so strong that we would give our lives for Him in a heartbeat? Would we just as readily give our lives for Him as He unhesitatingly gave His for us?

To Stand the Test

Right now, we may be able to stand for truth and for Jesus, its Author, in relative peace. But a time is surely coming—and quite likely far sooner than we suspect—when to stand for Jesus will be to invite the unreasoning wrath of those who oppose Him.

Against that day, are we deepening every day our commitment to our Lord? Are we building a will that can withstand any pressure to compromise, to yield, to save ourselves? Remember, though—a martyr's grace is not needed until or unless we face that choice. Focus now on strengthening love and commitment. If God calls any of us to make the ultimate sacrifice that so many Albigenses and Waldenses made, He will *then* and *only then* give us sufficient grace.

If you are deeply in love with a spouse here on earth—or if you are the parent of a child—you know that, were it necessary, to die for them would be a privilege and an honor. The same will be true of any of us whose love for our Creator runs too deep for words.

In every age, God has ALWAYS had a people—faithful and loyal, the called and chosen—and He still has a special people today.

CHAPTER 9

"HERE I STAND"

Ever lose your wallet or purse?

Chances are, you have. And chances are, when you have, people have tried to say helpful things.

Like: "Where did you see it last?"

Or: "Well, it didn't just grow legs and walk away."

Or: "Don't worry, it didn't just vanish into thin air."

At the moment, you may not consider these comments especially helpful. But they're true, nonetheless. Never in all the history of the world has a wallet grown legs and walked out the door. Not once. And never has a purse just evaporated from a solid into a gas. Never.

Which means that when something is lost, it still exists somewhere. It just needs to be found—to be recovered.

Jesus told stories of a lost coin, a lost sheep, a lost son. All three were ultimately found.

Divers look for the lost treasures of sunken ships that went down carrying loads of gold and jewels. Treasure hunters look for lost gold mines—or the staggering riches buried where the map is marked with an "x." Police look for lost children.

Restorers peel off the layers of later paintings to uncover a priceless art masterpiece underneath. Adventurers look for lost arks—whether the Ark of the Covenant or the Ark of Noah.

When things get lost, they are still there. They just need to be found again.

The greatest Treasure this world has ever known is not the Holy Grail or the Mines of Solomon or some as-yet-undiscovered field of diamonds the size of baseballs. The greatest Treasure ever present on Earth was its Creator: Jesus Christ. And when He left Earth, He also left to all His followers a treasure (small "t") that they could enjoy and share with others: His truth.

But over the years, this treasure of truth began to be covered by layers of error. This was no accident—it was the deliberate work of Christ's great enemy, who had infiltrated Christ's very own Church and led it to compromise and counterfeit and trample on the truth it had been given.

In time, every truth was buried under layers of error—falsehood, lies.

▶ The truth of salvation as a free gift was replaced with the false teaching of salvation by human effort.

▶ The truth of Jesus as our access to God was replaced with the doctrine of access only through human priests.

▶ The authority of the Bible was replaced by the authority of the Pope and of human tradition.

▶ Forgiveness was no longer a free gift to be received but a payment to be earned.

▶ The Sabbath day of rest was replaced by Sunday—a day of human choosing.

▶ Confession only to God was replaced by confession to priests.

▶ The Bible as God's gift to all was forbidden to be read or even possessed by any but Church leaders.

▸ Even the Ten Commandment Law of God was changed to suit a Church that had lost its way.

In addition, a host of nonbiblical teachings and practices were taught as "truth"—including the mass, transubstantiation (the supposed transformation of communion elements into Christ's literal body and blood), prayers for the dead, veneration of Mary and various "saints," and the sacredness of idols and images.

Remember that the single most important message of this book is this: God has *always* had faithful followers loyal to Him and to His truth. In every age since Eden, as Satan has done his best to hide or counterfeit or cover up truth, God has always had those determined to believe it, live it, and share it.

Whether the patriarchs following Adam, the faithful of Israel, the early Church believers, or those—such as the Albigenses and Waldenses we noted in the previous chapter, who stood for truth at the cost of their lives—God has always had an unbroken chain of the faithful.

At the darkest hours of the Dark Ages, God found brave and loyal ones determined to recover lost truth and bring it again into the open.

Bulletin Board Message

It began with a message on the campus bulletin board of a German university.

In those years, the door of the university church often served as the central message board for the campus—and on October 31, 1517, those who checked the door found a document posted by a Catholic priest and professor at the university. That document would change history, for Martin Luther's *95 Theses*—nailed to the door of Wittenberg's Castle Church—directly confronted error with Bible truth and launched the Protestant Reformation.

Though history marks Luther's *95 Theses* as the beginning of the Protestant Reformation, the truths that the Reformation would champion were set forth a century or more earlier by John Wycliffe. Though he died a hundred years before the birth of Martin Luther, he would later be known as the "Morningstar of the Reformation" for his bold teaching and preaching of Bible truth. Wycliffe's influence on later reformers such as Luther was profound, and he also would be known as the first to publish the Bible in the language of the common man and woman.

A student and follower of Wycliffe, John Hus, also had an enormous impact on the later reformers. He taught nearly all of the truths that Luther and others would later make the cornerstone of their efforts to reform a Church that had for centuries buried truth under layers of error.

Hus fearlessly opposed a variety of errors of the Church, including the sale of indulgences—the payment of fees or making of donations in order to secure forgiveness for sins. The Church branded Hus as a heretic, and in the year 1411, Hus was excommunicated from the Church. But he continued to teach Bible truth and oppose Church error, and finally, in 1415, the Church burned Hus at the stake. Jerome of Prague, a friend and follower of John Hus, would meet the same fate about a year later.

The Reformation Begins

These pre-Reformation leaders laid the foundation for the Reformation to follow. When Luther clearly drew the contrast between truth and error in 1517, the Reformation began in earnest. Soon, Luther found himself excommunicated from the Church. Assisted by the newly invented printing press, the movement spread rapidly. In Switzerland, Luther's efforts were echoed and joined by Ulrich Zwingli. The French theologian John Calvin brought together strands of the movement in Switzerland, Scotland, Hungary, Germany, and other points in Europe. The Dutch theologian Erasmus had a strong influence on Luther, and though he himself remained a member of the Catholic Church his entire life, he skillfully wrote out his opposition to its errors.

A key moment of the Reformation took place in the year 1521, when, on April 16, the Roman Emperor Charles V, in league with the Pope, summoned Luther to a Diet (assembly) in the city of Worms, Germany.

An assistant of a local archbishop, Johann Eck, directed Luther's attention to a table covered with copies of Luther's writings. Eck asked Luther if the books were his and if he still believed what he had written in them.

Luther asked for time before answering, which was granted. Luther thought, prayed, and consulted with his friends. The next day he returned to the Diet.

Eck now demanded that Luther answer the question: "Will you reject these books and the errors they contain?"

Luther's answer should be a matter of pride and challenge to every one of us who aspires to stand firm for the truths God has given us:

> "Unless I am convicted by Scripture and plain reason," Luther replied, "I do not accept the authority of popes and councils, for they have contradicted each other. My conscience is captive to the Word of God. I cannot and will not recant anything, for to go against conscience is neither right nor safe. Here I stand, I can do no other. God help me. Amen."

A few days later, the Diet issued an edict declaring Luther an outlaw and a heretic. But by this time, Luther had been safely spirited away by friends to Wartburg Castle. While there, Luther had opportunity to correspond and advise his friend and ally, Philipp Melanchthon. Melanchthon would be one of several who would later assist Luther in translating the Bible into German so the common people could have access to it.

This 1534 translation had a profound influence on William Tyndale, who subsequently published an English translation of the New Testament. Tyndale's work, in turn, would be foundational in the development of the King James Version of the Bible a few decades later.

Clearly, the Bible, locked away by the Church for centuries, was breaking free again. And as it did—as people could see the truth it taught in contrast with the errors taught by the Church—the work of reform raced forward.

Luther, the giant of the Reformation, would continue the work of recovering and restoring lost truths till his death in the year 1546.

Luther, Calvin, and other Reformation leaders stripped away centuries of lies and counterfeit teachings to bring to light the pure truths Jesus had originally entrusted to the early-church apostles and earliest Christians.

But the Reformation would in time lose its momentum and much of its original passion. Before *ALL* lost Bible truths could be found and restored, the reformed churches largely lost sight of their mission and occupied themselves with organizational questions and with debating their differences.

It would be the task of later Christians to restore other great lost truths, including the Sabbath, the second advent of Jesus, Christ's work as our Intercessor, and the truth about man's nature in life and in death.

Sardis

Of the seven churches in the Book of Revelation, the church of Reformation times is the church of Sardis. Note what God said to this church:

"And to the angel of the church in Sardis write, 'These things says He who has the seven Spirits of God and the seven stars: "I know your works, that you have a name that you are alive, but you are dead. Be watchful, and strengthen the things which remain, that are ready to die, for I have not found your works perfect before God. Remember therefore how you have received and heard; hold fast and repent. Therefore if you will not watch, I will come upon you as a thief, and you will not know what hour I will come upon you. You have a few names even in Sardis who have not defiled their garments; and they shall walk with Me in white, for they are worthy. He who overcomes shall be clothed in white garments, and I will not blot out his name from the Book of Life; but I will confess his name before My Father and before His angels."—Revelation 3:1-5.

Again, it's beyond the scope of this chapter to perform a detailed exposition of this message to Sardis. But notice at least two things:

"You have a name that you are alive, but you are dead," God told them. The Church appeared to be alive: constant services, dominance of both the religious and political worlds, an extensive priesthood, great wealth and ornate buildings.

But spiritually, it had long since died.

Then notice this: "You have a few names even in Sardis who have not defiled their garments; and they shall walk with Me in white, for they are worthy."

The few. The undefiled. The worthy. Yes, the same few we've been following all through time. The few who stayed loyal to Jesus and His truth no matter what.

These few included, of course, men like John Hus, Jerome of Prague, Luther, and so many others who boldly stood against error and proclaimed truth, no matter the cost. But it also included a host of unheralded, unrecorded believers who were no less courageous.

Among these were the Huguenots of France and Switzerland who responded with enthusiasm to the calls of Luther and Calvin for reform. They believed wholeheartedly in the keystone teachings of the Reformation: salvation through faith, the authority of the Bible, and direct access to God through Jesus, not human priests.

Aggressive in their opposition to the Catholic Church and its teachings and practices, the Huguenots soon felt the wrath of persecution. The French Wars of Religion against them began with a massacre in March of 1562 at which an unknown number of Huguenots were killed.

In what became known as the St. Bartholomew's Day Massacre of August 24 through September 17 of 1572, the slaughter that began in Paris and spread to surrounding towns resulted in the deaths of an estimated 70,000 Huguenots. Persecution continued against them until 1598, when Henry IV, a new king of France, granted them religious and political freedom, but only in their own territories.

In the 1600s, many Huguenots migrated to South Africa, as well as to the thirteen colonies of North America. Among these was a silversmith named Apollos Rivoire, who gave his anglicized name and profession to his son, Paul Revere—the famed American revolutionary.

Today as you read these chapters, we enjoy the privilege of living and teaching our faith in virtually complete freedom. But we also live in a world that is changing before our very eyes. A world where personal freedoms seem increasingly at risk in the service of national security.

We will not always have the freedoms we've known so long that we've come to take for granted. A time is coming when once again, opposition and even persecution will arise.

Will we be among the faithful few then?

The best way to know that answer now is to be sure of our faithfulness now. Is our faith rooted in principle and commitment—or is it a matter of convenience? Is our allegiance only to a set of truths—or is it first of all to the Truth? Jesus said, "I am the Way, the Truth, and the Life"—John 14:6.

If we love Truth, we will love the truth.

If we are loyal to Truth, we will be loyal to the truth.

A parting question for this chapter: Shall we fear the possibility of persecution? Or when it comes—as it will—shall we not rather welcome the opportunity to stand loyal to Jesus as the greatest of all honors and privileges?

In every age, God has ALWAYS had a people—faithful and loyal, the called and chosen—and He still has a special people today.

CHAPTER 10

FROM THE ASHES, TRIUMPH

No matter how long the relay race—no matter how many runners one thing stays the same from beginning to end: the baton.

From first runner to last, the baton is passed from one to the next.

First passed from Adam, the baton has been carried down through the centuries by a succession of the loyal—and it will arrive securely when the long race ends at the second coming of Jesus.

The baton? It is the Good News of The Truth, Jesus Christ—and of His truth: what He shared with the world during His life and what He continues to share in His Word.

Century to century, the baton was passed:

▸ From Adam and the Old Testament patriarchs...to Israel and its prophets.

▸ From Israel...to the early Christian Church.

▸ From the early Church...to the Church of the long, Dark Ages.

▶ From that Church in the Wilderness...to the brave leaders of the Reformation.

▶ And from the Reformers...to the leaders of the Great Second Advent Movement.

The Protestant Reformation brought long-neglected and deliberately suppressed truths back into the light of day. It exposed a Church that had sold out to the great enemy, replacing truth with error and lies—and persecuting those who refused to surrender loyalty to save themselves.

Dedicated men helped carry the baton of truth during the Reformation and move it forward: men like Luther and Zwingli and Calvin and Melanchthon. But so did thousands of faithful men and women whose names no one knows.

For a reason that will become clear momentarily, this brings us to the subject of tunnels.

Currently the longest tunnel in the world, Japan's Seikan Tunnel between the islands of Honshu and Hokkaido—a railway tunnel—is 31 miles long. Under construction in Switzerland, the Gotthard Base Tunnel, scheduled for completion in 2012, will be 35 miles long.

Imagine entering a tunnel in Chicago, Illinois, in the United States—and driving all the way to Miami, Florida—a distance of 1,186 miles—and never emerging from the tunnel. Imagine a tunnel 1,260 miles long. A dark, dangerous tunnel plagued with frequent cave-ins and marauding bands of lawless gang members.

In A.D. 538, God's true followers entered a tunnel measured not in miles but in years—a tunnel that moved through time for 1,260 years. A tunnel of oppression and persecution by the dominant but apostate Roman Church. A tunnel known as the Dark Ages, with only the Word of God to light the way.

But in A.D. 1798, the power of the papacy came to an end

with the capture of the pope of Rome by the French general Berthier—an event described in Revelation 13:3 as a "deadly wound."

From 1517, when Luther posted his 95 *Theses* on the door of Wittenberg's Castle Church, to 1798, the Reformation moved forward—a time of recovering long-lost, long-suppressed truth.

But even as the Reformation lost much of its momentum in the sands of institutionalism and denominationalism, humble seekers both in Europe and America continued to search the Word of God to find even more truth.

And the great truth to emerge from this search could not have been more timely. For in only four short decades, a great movement swept the religious world, centered on the electrifying news from God's Word that the second advent of Jesus Christ was near.

Spanning the Atlantic from Europe to America, scores of prophetic scholars reached this same conclusion, and the Great Second Advent Movement swept through the churches with astonishing results.

But in America, the central personality of this movement was no seminary-trained scholar. He was not the famed pastor of an influential city church. He was, in fact, a man who began his own spiritual journey with a rather dim—or at least limited—view of God.

The Young Deist

Born into a Christian home, William Miller as a young man abandoned his early beliefs in favor of deism—the religious philosophy that God is basically an absentee landlord, that He may originally have wound up the world like a watch, but that He then walked off to let it run on its own. Such a God, said deism, doesn't take a personal interest in His creation and certainly never performs miracles.

When his uncle and grandfather, both Baptist clergymen, would occasionally visit William to labor with him concerning his beliefs, he would afterward entertain his friends by mocking them.

But after a close brush with death as he served in the War of 1812, William began to review his deistic beliefs. He returned to his upstate New York boyhood home in Low Hampton and took up the vocation shared by nine of ten in America at that time—farming. His doubts about deism deepened, and his hunger for the peace of a personal Saviour grew more intense.

Searching His Bible, he found the Saviour he was seeking. But now, just as he had taunted his uncle and grandfather after their visits, his unbelieving friends taunted him, assuring him that the Bible was full of contradictions.

"If the Bible is the Word of God," he responded, "then everything it contains can be understood, and all its parts made to harmonize. Give me time, and I'll harmonize its apparent contradictions, or I'll be a Deist still."

The Bible and a Concordance

As an Adventist, you know well what happened next. Miller set aside every book he owned except for the Bible and Cruden's *Concordance*, and, beginning at Genesis 1, began to work his way through the Word. He determined not to move ahead any faster than he could resolve any problems or seeming contradictions that he encountered. His method was to let the Bible explain itself.

One after another, the apparent inconsistencies of the Word fell away. And chapter by chapter, Miller found his friendship with Jesus growing stronger and deeper.

Verse by verse, he forged ahead, till one day, he arrived at the verse that would capture his lifelong attention—and launch a movement that would likewise capture the attention of a still-young American nation of only seventeen million.

Daniel 8:14: "Unto two thousand and three hundred days; then shall the sanctuary be cleansed."

Miller's study became all-consuming, sometimes lasting entire nights. Comparing scripture with scripture, he discovered that in time prophecies, a day in the Bible stands for a year. So the 2,300 days were 2,300 years. Further study of Daniel, chapters 8 and 9, led Miller to conclude that the 2,300 years began in 457 B.C., which meant, he calculated, that they would end in 1843—a scant twenty-five years into the future.

And the cleansing of the sanctuary, Miller concluded, was the personal return of Jesus Christ to this earth at His second advent. In his very soul, Miller heard a voice saying, "Go, and tell it to the world."

For five more years, Miller evaded this inner call by studying more deeply his discovery—checking and double-checking his conclusions. When these years of research removed all doubts, a new deterrent arose: fear of public speaking. For another eight years, Miller resisted the inner call he felt to share his discoveries through preaching. But the inner voice grew more insistent.

So on a Saturday morning, Miller struck a "bargain" with God that he was certain would remove the burden. "O Lord," he said, "I will enter into a covenant with You. If you send me an invitation to preach on these things, then I'll go."

In great relief, Miller settled into his chair. No one was about to ask a 50-year-old uneducated farmer to preach on the second coming.

Wrong. Someone *WAS* about to.

Within thirty minutes, a loud knocking at his door roused Miller.

"Good morning to you, Uncle William," said the boy at the door.

"Nephew Irving!" Miller exclaimed. "And what might you

be doing sixteen miles from home so early in the morning?"

"Uncle William, I left before breakfast to tell you that our Baptist minister in Dresden is unable to speak at services tomorrow. Father sent me to make a request of you. He wants you to come and talk to us about the things you've been studying in the Bible—about the second coming of Christ, you know. Will you come?"

Struggle in the Maple Grove

Miller turned on his heel without a word, left Irving standing there in confusion, and stormed out the door and over to a nearby maple grove. There, for a solid hour, he fought with God with no less energy than Jacob fought with the Angel of the Old Testament.

William Miller was angry with himself for making his covenant with God. He was also petrified. He begged and pled with God to send someone else. But finally after tears and anquish, he gave in to God—and the surrender brought both peace and happiness. So filled with joy now was Miller that he began hopping up and down, praising God out loud. His young daughter Lucy Ann, watching anxiously from the door, rushed into the house. "Mother, Mother—come quick!"

Soon Miller and Irving were on their way to Dresden. So moved were the people at Dresden that they persuaded Miller to preach every night for a week.

From the beginning, other invitations poured in from people who had heard of his messages in Dresden. From nearly every denomination, the urgent requests came to him like a steadily growing avalanche.

Wherever Miller preached, revivals followed. Whole towns were transformed by his amazing news that the second coming of Jesus was so very, very near. For eight years, Miller was kept constantly busy preaching in one small town after another. Then, in the fall of 1839 after a meeting in Exeter, New Hampshire, he met a young man who would change the course of his ministry.

Joshua V. Himes was only 34 years of age, but he was already well known for his public opposition to slavery, liquor, and war. After the Exeter service, Himes introduced himself and invited Miller to preach at Himes' chapel on Chardon Street in Boston, Massachusetts.

So it came about that on December 8, 1839, Miller preached his first series in a major American city. Even with two services a day, hundreds had to be turned away.

"Do you really believe what you've been preaching to us?" Himes asked Miller one night.

"I most certainly do, Brother Himes, or I would not be preaching it."

"Then what are you doing to spread it to the world?"

When Miller protested that he had done all he could to reach every little town and village to which he had been invited, Himes was aghast.

Every little town and village?

What about the cities? What about Baltimore, and New York, and Philadelphia? What about the entire seventeen million citizens of the United States?

"If Christ is coming in just a few years as you believe," Himes said, "then there is no time to lose in sending out the message in thundertones to arouse them to prepare."

Himes, afire with a vision for what needed to be done, became the facilitator, the planner, the organizer. Soon, he had lined up appointments for Miller in the largest cities of the country, and soon, Miller's name was known everywhere.

Himes persuaded the pastors of his own denomination, the Christian Connexion, to open their pulpits to Miller. In one of these churches, Miller's message reached the Robert Harmon family—and thus it was that their teen-aged daughter Ellen, a future founder of the Seventh-day Adventist Church, found and gave her life to the advent hope.

Like wildfire, the movement spread. Himes, always energetic, began a publishing ministry to accompany Miller's spoken messages. Other ministers too joined the movement to add their efforts. Josiah Litch, a Methodist, published a 200-page book on Miller's lectures. Litch also helped persuade Charles Fitch, a Boston Congregationalist pastor, to assist. Litch and another well-known Methodist, Apollos Hale, developed what became known as the "1843 Chart," summarizing the prophetic timeline central to Miller's messages.

But the "Millerite movement" had grown far beyond just one man. The Great Second Advent Movement now swept through the churches of North America like a tsunami. Camp meetings and conferences drew thousands.

Miller had long avoided becoming too specific about the exact time of Christ's return, his message stating only that Jesus would return "about the year 1843." But by January of that year, he had concluded, based on additional research—and taking into account the Jewish year—that Jesus would return sometime between March 21, 1843, and March 21, 1844.

When the full year passed, and Jesus had not returned, a first great disappointment settled over the movement. But later in 1844—at an August camp meeting in Exeter, New Hampshire, the movement gained a new lease with the discoveries shared there by a Millerite minister named S. S. Snow. His study of Daniel's prophecy of the 2,300 days led him to conclude that Jesus would return on the tenth day of the seventh Jewish month, which in 1844 would fall on October 22—only two months away.

The electrifying news triggered an epidemic of enthusiasm. People left the camp meeting to spread the word: "Behold, the Bridegroom cometh!" Soon, Miller, Himes, and the other movement leaders agreed that Snow's reckoning most certainly was right.

On October 22, 1844, tens of thousands of believers waited for their Lord to appear. But when the day came and went, this second disappointment was shattering and too deep for words.

On October 24, Litch wrote to Miller: "It is a cloudy and dark day here—the sheep are scattered—and the Lord has not yet come."

Aftermath

After the Great Disappointment, some believers lost all hope and abandoned either the movement or their Christian allegiance—or both. Some concluded that nothing at all had happened on October 22—that they had completely misinterpreted scripture. Others decided that Jesus *had* come on October 22, but that His coming was an invisible, *spiritual* coming. Still others fell into lengthy, inconsolable depression. And some few continued to pray and search, convinced that somehow, they had missed something in their understanding of the Bible.

As every Adventist now knows, from this latter group emerged a small number of earnest Bible students who concluded that something indeed had happened on October 22, 1844—but that rather than the second coming of Jesus, what had happened was the entrance of Jesus into the Most Holy Place of the sanctuary in heaven, to begin His last intercessory ministry.

Men such as Hiram Edson, O. R. L. Crosier, and F. B. Hahn concluded that the sanctuary to be cleansed was not the earth—but the sanctuary in heaven.

Soon others would join these men in their study and join them in their conclusions. Among them: a young Christian

Connexion pastor named James White; the teen-aged daughter of the Harmon family—Ellen Harmon, now James White's wife; and a retired sea captain named Joseph Bates.

From the ashes of bitter disappointment would arise a movement that would extend the Great Second Advent Movement far beyond its original scope. From the tears of disillusionment would arise a new certainty based on the Word of God that would give rise to a people charged with giving God's last, urgent call to an unsuspecting world that the coming of Jesus was indeed, even at the doors!

Of Revelation's seven churches, the church extending from the Reformation through the Second Advent Movement was the church of Philadelphia—the Church of "brotherly love." But as God's final people began to arise—to be called out from the confused Babylon of other churches—the seventh and final Church would follow: the Church of Laodicea. And God would have strong warnings and rebukes for this Church, as we shall see in the chapter to follow.

The unbroken chain of God's faithful? Most surely, during the decades of the Great Second Advent Movement, it included leaders such as Miller and Himes and Fitch—and later Edson and the Whites and Bates.

But yes, as always, it also included the great host of the unnamed faithful—those loyal to the truth—and to Truth—no matter what.

The race has been long. From Adam onward, the baton has been passed. With the advent movement, the baton passes now into your hands, and mine.

We are now on the final leg of the relay.

That baton is in your hand, my friend—so grip it firmly. It has traveled far. On it are the fingerprints of Adam, and Noah, and Daniel and Joseph and David—of Paul and Peter and John—of the Waldenses and Albigenses and Huguenots—of

Luther and Calvin and Zwingli and Wycliffe—of Miller and
Himes and Edson and White.

Where will it now travel in your hands?

> *In every age, God has ALWAYS had a people—faithful and
> loyal, the called and chosen—and He still has
> a special people today.*

CHAPTER 11

CHAMPIONS OF TRUTH

Ever get lost driving around in a large city?

Now, ideally, the way to find your location would be to just magically rise up into the air high enough so you could look down on a much larger area and see where you are. But floating into the sky to get your bearings isn't really a practical option.

No problem, though, if you happen to live in America, Europe, Australia—or some other area of the world where you've been able to get one of those relatively new GPS units in your car. With a GPS (ground positioning system), you don't have to rise high into the sky, because a network of satellites are already up there—12,000 miles up, in fact—and by "triangulating" or "comparing notes" amongst themselves, they can "see" exactly where you are.

With a GPS receiver in your car, you can not only see on a screen where you are but get directions to anywhere you want to go. For anyone who is "directionally challenged," a GPS can be a genuine blessing!

Sometimes, it's possible you can get "lost" even in reading a book. You can turn left onto one topic, right on another, then travel several miles through a series of paragraphs and chapters, and sort of forget where you started and where you're going.

So perhaps it's time now to stop for a moment and get our bearings again. Let's review where we started, where we've been, and where we'll still be going.

We began this book by noting that its purpose is to tell a story—the story of God's loyal followers through the centuries. These followers of God have accepted a specific mission from Him—to be champions of truth.

And that truth is twofold. It includes all the truth God has shared through His Word—and all the truth taught and lived out by Jesus during His life on earth. But part of all this truth is the most important of all—the truth about God's character.

The great enemy says God can't be trusted—that He lies, that He demands the impossible, that He is judgmental, vengeful, and determined to take away our freedom and destroy our happiness. The enemy says God is responsible for all the suffering and misery and death on Planet Earth—that He is to blame when bad things happen in our lives. And the enemy says that if only he were in charge of the universe, everyone would find ultimate happiness.

Even many Christian leaders today present God to the world as eager to visit judgment and destruction on those who sin. So if a great tidal wave or cyclone or earthquake claims thousands of lives, it has to be because God is angry with sinners and is hurling down His judgments.

And the enemy takes it a step further: not only does God destroy people for not keeping His law, but He does so knowing that they *can't* keep it—since He has made a law that's impossible to keep.

What is God really like? Is He a God of love—or a God of stern judgment and destruction? Did He make a law He knew nobody could keep—then condemn them to death when they failed to keep it? Does He hold out the carrot of heaven and eternal life as a reward for good behavior, only to apply the stick of punishment when we behave badly? When He asks us to love Him, is it "Love me—*or else?*"

The Counterfeiter

For every truth God has ever shared with the human beings He created, the enemy has created a counterfeit. Sin is deadly, God warned. Stay away from it—it will kill you. Not so, said Satan. "You will *not* surely die!" No, after you "die," your soul lives on. You're still alive—just in another dimension.

The seventh day is the Sabbath, God said. Not so, said Satan. It's Sunday—the *first* day of the week.

When Jesus comes, every eye will see Him, the Bible told us. Not so, said Satan. Jesus will come secretly, in a rapture, and only a few will see Him.

The lies go on and on. Why? Because Satan's rebellion against God was so complete that he no longer *can* tell the truth. He can only lie.

So for every truth God has ever shared with us, Satan has a lie that has become the accepted teaching of the great majority of even Christians on earth.

But Satan doesn't stop with lying about what God *taught* us. He is actually far more interested in lying about who *God is*.

But from the beginning, God has always had a people who refused to accept the enemy's lies—even when taught by those who also claimed to be God's followers. From the beginning, He has had loyal followers who not only championed the truths God shared with the human race but the Truth God shared with the human race—the One who called Himself "The Way, the *Truth*, and the Life."

When Jesus was here, He said, "He who has seen Me has

seen the Father" (John 14:9). Jesus, the Truth, came not only to share *truths* with us—but to share also the truth about His Father.

- ▶ Adam and the patriarchs championed truths—and the Truth.

- ▶ Israel and her prophets and kings championed truths—and the Truth.

- ▶ The early Church championed truths—and the Truth.

- ▶ Besieged by persecution and compromise, believers in the early centuries after the apostles championed truths—and the Truth.

- ▶ Battling an apostate Church, the Reformers championed truths—and the Truth.

- ▶ Post-reformation Bible students in Europe and America focused on the second coming of Jesus and championed truths—and the Truth.

Then came that bitter disappointment when Jesus did not return. But out of that great heartbreak would arise what Adventist historian L. E. Froom would call a "movement of destiny"—one last, final remnant of God's loyal who would champion His truths—and the Truth.

Unbroken Chain

So in our pause in this chapter to "get our bearings," we see that from Eden onward, a steady, unbroken chain of the loyal and faithful have continued through century after century to this present moment. And we see that the mission of God's true followers has never changed. It is to share and champion His truths—so savagely and shamefully counterfeited by the great enemy. And it is to share and champion even more fervently the Truth—the Lord and Saviour of us all, Jesus Christ.

The Reformation recovered many long-suppressed, long-lost truths. It also exposed centuries of error and lies and counterfeits. Among its greatest gifts to the world were its insistence on the authority of the Bible—not human tradition—and on salvation by faith in Jesus—not by faith in human effort and merit.

But the Reformation lost its momentum before it could be complete. Other vital truths remained to be reclaimed. The great advent awakening rediscovered and championed the truth of Christ's Second Advent, despite its initial misunderstandings of Bible prophecy.

Now, like the runners in a relay race we noted earlier in this book, the baton was about to be passed to the final runner. God would call forth one final, remnant people to champion His truths—and His Truth—in the final years of earth's history. He would give this final runner the most important assignment of all.

Yes, this final group of His loyal—this final remnant—would recover many lost or neglected truths: the Sabbath, Christ's ministry in the heavenly sanctuary, the nature of man in life and death, and yes, the imminence of Christ's return to this earth.

But He would also give the final remnant the three most vital, most urgent messages ever shared with the world: the messages of three angels as found in the prophecies of the book of Revelation.

These three messages presented in Revelation 14:6-12 are God's last appeal—and His last warning—to the billions living on this earth as time runs out its final years and hours. Just as Noah appealed to and warned the world of His time, and just as John the Baptist appealed to and warned the world before Christ's first coming, God has a people whose task and privilege it is to appeal to and warn the world of A.D. 2000 and beyond that Jesus is almost here.

Briefly, the three angels' messages of Revelation are:

1. The everlasting gospel, made urgent because of the judgment hour.

2. God's call to His people to come out of the confused Babylon of counterfeit religions.

3. A warning that to linger too long in false religion is to risk receiving the "mark" of the "beast" of the great enemy.

Yes, there are urgent warnings here. Yes, it is necessary for God's final remnant to clearly contrast truths with errors and counterfeits. But notice that the three messages begin with the "everlasting gospel." Nothing else is more important. It is Priority One. Telling the world the truth about God—made too clear to miss in the life and death of Jesus—is the *primary* task of God's last true followers.

"Of all professing Christians," Ellen White wrote, "Seventh-day Adventists should be foremost in uplifting Christ before the world"—*Gospel Workers,* p. 156.

So what about all the doctrines and truths that from 1844's disappointment to the present day have been recovered, rediscovered, and reclaimed by God's remnant? Next to the *Truth,* are *truths* not so important?

Hardly. For what is the Source of all that truth? Who taught them?

But we do need to guard against two great mistakes.

The first is to look around us and assume that since other churches do not teach these truths but apparently focus on Jesus and salvation, that we should leave that to them and spend our greatest effort on sharing the unique doctrinal truths God has led us to discover.

The second mistake is to present these truths as if they stood alone and on their own. For no *truth*—no doctrine—is correct or even understandable, unless it is seen in its connection to the *Truth*. All doctrines, all truths, begin and end with

Jesus. The Sabbath is important only for what it says about Jesus—for how it helps us understand His character of love. The sanctuary isn't just symbols and services, it is a tangible illustration of how the love of Jesus saves us.

At least some of the confused religions of this world teach and preach Jesus. But they so easily leave the tracks and teach "cheap grace," or "once-saved, always saved," or that some are predestined to be saved and others to be lost.

God has given His final remnant the clearest, most balanced and accurate understanding of salvation ever revealed to the human race. In addition, He has shown how every teaching, every doctrine of the Bible says something about Jesus—how each of these truths helps us understand what God is really like.

The Remnant

As an Adventist—either recently baptized or a member from childhood—you have perhaps often heard of "the remnant." That isn't a marketing slogan voted by some church committee. It's God's own description of His final, faithful followers.

Notice Revelation 12:17 (KJV): "And the dragon was wroth with the woman, and went to make war with the remnant of her seed, which keep the commandments of God, and have the testimony of Jesus Christ."

The dragon, Satan, this prophecy says, was angry with "the woman"—God's true followers, His church—and went to make war on "the remnant" of her seed. Remnant: that which remains. The final part.

And this remnant, the prophecy says, can be identified by two things: 1) They keep the commandments of God, and 2) they have the "testimony of Jesus Christ."

We'll be looking more closely at these two identifying marks of the remnant in an upcoming chapter. But for now, a caution.

It would be so easy to conclude that the Seventh-day Adventist Church—the "movement of destiny" of which Dr. Froom wrote—is the exclusive home of God's only true people—and that only by membership in the Church can salvation be assured.

But aside from the fact that the Bible is clear that salvation comes not through church membership but by faith in Christ alone, the fact is that not all of God's true "remnant"—His loyal followers—are yet a part of the Adventist Church.

"Notwithstanding the spiritual darkness and alienation from God that exist in the churches which constitute Babylon," Ellen White wrote, "the great body of Christ's true followers are still to be found in their communion"—*The Great Controversy*, p. 390.

Does this mean that the Seventh-day Adventist Church is not God's remnant? Not at all. But not all of God's remnant *people* are yet in His remnant *Church.* In fact, some of those remnant people may have died—or may yet pass on—without ever having had the chance officially to join the remnant church.

But if God is going to say, "Come out of Babylon," He is also going to say, "Come into the remnant!" And this remnant is the fellowship of the called-out—the organization of the commissioned to carry out God's final assignment. God didn't create the remnant to offer salvation as a benefit of membership. He created His remnant Church to be a place where God's loyal followers could come together to learn how to join their efforts in becoming champions of His truths—and of the One who *is* Truth.

Have you ever wrestled with a rope or cord or even a garden hose that seemed hopelessly tangled? How do you ultimately get it untangled? You have to find one of the ends, and begin from there.

We Adventists sometimes spend a lot of time and effort and even argument, trying to untangle things. We debate church standards, we nitpick theology, we argue about how to apply the *Church Manual,* we dissect doctrines.

So much time could be saved—and so much greater could be our effectiveness—if when things seem tangled, we'd just reflexively go back to find an "end." For everything—every doctrine, every church standard, every church practice—begins and ends with Jesus Christ. If we would only start there—and end there—the tangles would disappear. We would find harmony with each other—and stop majoring in minors.

We have an urgent, absolutely vital task to do. We have a Savior to lift up to those around us. We have truths to share. We have errors to warn against. We have the return of Christ to announce.

It's no accident that you are a Seventh-day Adventist. You've been called out and chosen. Yes, you. God has invited you to take your place in the long line of His faithful. He has asked you to pick up the baton and run the final leg of the race. He has asked you to be a champion for truth—and for Truth.

So go to class today. Go to work. Do your errands. Take care of your children. Live the life you're "in." But be available to God today. Be His channel. Be His voice. Let His love flow through you to the lost and confused and the searching. Believe in the "divine appointments" He creates for you. Stay prepared to share.

Imagine how God has honored you—how privileged you are—to be part of His last "movement of destiny." The more we share Him and His truth with those around us, the sooner we'll see His face!

In every age, God has ALWAYS had a people—faithful and loyal, the called and chosen—and He still has a special people today.

CHAPTER 12

A GIFT LIKE NO OTHER

"What is that in your hand?" God asked Moses.

▸ A rod. A simple wooden rod. But with it, Moses would deliver Israel.

▸ In the hands of three hundred men, God used trumpets, torches, and clay jars to help Gideon and his band rout the Midianites.

▸ In the hands of Jesus, five loaves and two fishes fed five thousand.

God often uses the simple, the humble, the apparently weak.

As the Seventh-day Adventist Church began emerging from the ashes of the Great Disappointment of 1844, God used a teen-aged girl to become His chosen messenger to the remnant.

Ellen Harmon—born in 1827—received a vision of God's people on their journey to heaven, when she was just 17 years old. This would be just the first of about 2,000 visions she would receive during her lifetime of ministry. In 1846, Ellen married James White, a young minister who shared with her the conviction that Jesus was soon to return. Soon after their marriage, James and Ellen also accepted the Bible truth of the seventh-day Sabbath.

Ellen and her husband James, along with retired sea captain Joseph Bates, are considered the primary founders of the Seventh-day Adventist Church, which was organized in the year 1863.

Adventist readers know that Mrs. White—or "Sister White," as she is also known in the Church—was a prolific author of over forty books and 5,000 periodical articles. Since her death in 1915, many other books have been published from her previously unpublished material as well as compiled from her published works. Today more than one hundred of her books are in print in the English language, and she is the most-translated female American author of all time.

During her long ministry, she was personally instrumental in helping establish the Church's medical, publishing, and educational ministries. And of course, her published counsels—many based on her visions—helped guide the young Church in its early years, as they continue to do today.

From the beginning, Adventist believers have been convinced that Mrs. White possessed the true biblical gift of prophecy. They also believe that Revelation 12:17 and 19:10 set forth the presence of this prophetic gift as one of the two identifying marks of God's final, remnant people.

Though Ellen White herself never claimed to be a prophet, referring to herself instead as "the Lord's messenger," in applying the biblical tests of a prophet to Mrs. White and her writings, Adventists are convinced that she possessed the genuine Bible gift of prophecy.

In brief summary form, here are the key tests the Bible gives us for determining whether or not a person possesses the genuine gift of prophecy:

1. The test of fulfilled predictions—Jer. 28:9: "As for the prophet who prophesies of peace, when the word of the prophet comes to pass, the prophet will be known as one whom the Lord has truly sent."

This Bible test must also include the principle of "conditional" prophecy—acknowledging that some prophecies depend for their fulfillment on the response of God's people. Again, it is Jeremiah who sets forth this principle:

"The instant I speak concerning a nation and concerning a kingdom, to pluck up, to pull down, and to destroy it, if that nation against whom I have spoken turns from its evil, I will relent of the disaster that I thought to bring upon it. And the instant I speak concerning a nation and concerning a kingdom, to build and to plant it, if it does evil in My sight so that it does not obey My voice, then I will relent concerning the good with which I said I would benefit it"—Jer. 18:7-10.

2. The test of agreement with the Bible—Isa. 8:20: "To the law and to the testimony! If they do not speak according to this word, it is because there is no light in them." In Bible times—as well as in later centuries—the sum total of all earlier prophetic, scriptural writings was the benchmark by which each successive prophet's messages were measured. Though later prophets might provide new insights into God's truths, these concepts would never contradict the foundational truths already revealed by earlier biblical prophets.

3. The test of fruit-bearing—Matt. 7:15-20: "Beware of false prophets, who come to you in sheep's clothing, but inwardly they are ravenous wolves. You will know them by their fruits. Do men gather grapes from thornbushes or figs from thistles? Even so, every good tree bears good fruit, but a bad tree bears bad fruit. A good tree cannot bear bad fruit, nor can a bad tree bear good fruit. . . . Therefore by their fruits you will know them."

This test—unlike the first two—takes time, as fruit does not develop and ripen overnight. But as a prophet's character, ministry, and messages become more evident, a careful evaluation will increasingly reveal whether this fruit is what the prophetic tree is expected to bear.

4. The test of bearing witness to the divine-human nature of Jesus Christ—1 John 4:1-3: "Beloved, do not believe every spirit, but test the spirits, whether they are of God; because many false prophets have gone out into the world. By this you know the Spirit of God: Every spirit that confesses that Jesus Christ has come in the flesh is of God, and every spirit that does not confess that Jesus Christ has come in the flesh is not of God."

A true prophet does not just acknowledge that Jesus once lived on earth. True prophets profess and communicate that Jesus was fully God—and fully man. The incarnation of Jesus is central to the ministry and outreach of a true prophet.

5. The source test—true prophets do not manufacture their own prophecies but present to others only what the Holy Spirit reveals to them—2 Pet. 1:21: "For prophecy never came by the will of man, but holy men of God spoke as they were moved by the Holy Spirit."

Likewise, true prophets do not provide their own personal or private interpretation of prophecy. Instead, they rely on scripture to provide the interpretation. "Knowing this first, that no prophecy of Scripture is of any private interpretation"—2 Pet. 1:20.

From the earliest days of the Advent movement to the present moment, hundreds, then thousands, and finally, millions have studied the life and messages of Ellen G. White and measured her ministry by these Bible tests of a true prophet. In each decade, the conclusion has been the same: Ellen White indeed evidenced in her life and in her speaking and writing the marks of a true prophet.

But how, some may ask, do Mrs. White's writings relate to

the Bible? Are they an *addition* to the Bible? If so, how does that idea fit with the Reformation truth of the Bible—and the Bible alone?

In the early years of the Church, Adventists had to sort out these questions. In 1863, pioneer editor and author Uriah Smith wrote an article in the church journal—the *Review and Herald*—entitled "Do We Discard the Bible By Endorsing the Visions?" In it, he focused on this key principle of the Reformation: "The Bible—and the Bible Alone."

The Harbor Pilot

Elder Smith's article used the illustration of an ocean liner nearing its destination port. According to the ship's manual, just prior to entering the port, the vessel is instructed to stop and let a harbor pilot board—a pilot who knows the treacherous waters ahead.

"The gifts of the Spirit," he wrote, "are given for our pilot through these perilous times, and wherever and in whomsoever we find genuine manifestations of these, we are bound to respect them, nor can we do otherwise without in so far rejecting the Word of God, which directs us to receive them. Who now stand upon the Bible, and the Bible alone?"—*Review and Herald*, Jan. 13, 1863.

As the remnant Church approaches port, the Bible says this remnant will be given a "pilot"—the gift of prophecy—to guide it through the final perilous waters of the journey.

If that is in fact what the Bible says—and we have already found in Revelation that it is—then who, Elder Smith asked, really believes in the Bible and the Bible only—those who accept the pilot, or those who don't?

Ellen White herself never saw her writings as an addition to the Bible, but as a "lesser light leading to the greater light." Just as Jesus came to reveal the Father, and just as the Spirit lifts up Jesus, her prophetic writings lift up and honor the Bible.

Other churches, of course, also have their prophets—or in-spired books. But there are major differences. The Mormons—the Church of Jesus Christ of Latter-Day Saints—which arose about the same time as did Seventh-day Adventists, has its Book of Mormon and other books they consider inspired. These books, they consider as on the same level as the Bible—and as an addition to it. The same is true of the Apocrypha, which the Roman Catholic Church considers as fully a part of scripture as the Bible itself.

The writings of Ellen White—which Adventists also call "The Spirit of Prophecy" writings—are seen more like a mag-nifying glass or bright lamp that illuminates the Bible to make it easier to see and understand its truths.

There is another large difference between Adventists and other churches that claim prophets or inspired writings. Cath-olics, for example, consider papal decrees and church tradi-tions as *above* the Bible—they take precedence over it even if these two sources are not in agreement. But Adventists believe that all gifts and manifestations of the Spirit must be evaluated by the Bible—and that anything that is not in harmony with the Word cannot be accepted.

Why the Prophetic Gift?

So how should we see the role of the Spirit of Prophecy in the Church? What is its purpose? Why did God think the Church would need it? Consider these suggestions:

1. Just as God's small band of the loyal through the centuries championed the suppressed and neglected truths of the Bible, the Spirit of Prophecy focuses light on truths God is restoring in these final days of human history: the Sabbath, the sanctuary, the state of the dead, the second coming, and the great truth of righteousness by faith in Jesus.

But let us never accept the accusation of some that Adventists developed their doctrines—assembled their body of truths—by relying primarily on the writings and visions of Ellen White.

For example, early critics claimed that the doctrine of the heavenly sanctuary was developed and based primarily on the visions of Mrs. White. In 1874, Elder Uriah Smith—at the time the editor of the *Review and Herald,* met this charge in an editorial:

> "Hundreds of articles have been written on the subject. But in no one of these are the visions once referred to as any authority on this subject, or the source from whence any view we hold has been derived. . . . The appeal is invariably to the Bible, where there is abundant evidence for the views we hold on this subject"—*Review and Herald,* Dec, 22, 1874.

A careful investigation of our early history as a Church will show that the same words Elder Smith wrote concerning the sanctuary truth would apply to *all* the truths Adventists discovered as they searched the Word. Often, however, after early Adventist Bible students uncovered a significant Bible truth by long hours of study and prayer, that truth would be "confirmed" as true and important in a vision presented to Mrs. White. And in the years that followed, the writings of Mrs. White would elevate and honor and emphasize the importance of those truths.

2. The Spirit of Prophecy is of enormous value to Adventists in their mission to tell the truth about God and His character of love. In the great controversy between Christ and Satan, the enemy devoted himself to attacking the character of God. It has always been the privilege of God's true followers to defend and tell the truth about the kind of God who rules this universe. And as the controversy arrives at its final battles, that mission—now the task of the remnant—has never been more urgent or critical.

God is *not* the Author of suffering and death and misery.

God is *not* the destroyer.

God is *not* a vengeful judge out to catch us doing wrong.

God is *not* the Author of a law that He knows is impossible to keep.

In language that is elegant and eloquent, Ellen White wrote the truth about God—and what she wrote in books such as *Steps to Christ, The Desire of Ages,* and *Christ's Object Lessons* paints a picture of God that Adventists can eagerly share with those who have been deceived by Satan's lies.

3. The Spirit of Prophecy clearly tells the full story of the great controversy. Do you realize that no other church, no other religious group on earth, teaches or even understands the heart of the Bible's story—the great controversy theme? It is unique to Seventh-day Adventists, and it is our great privilege to share it with those who haven't yet heard or understood it. The "great controversy theme" is the big picture. It is the overarching story of the cosmic contest between good and evil. It is the view of the entire forest that shows the important place of each individual tree.

The great controversy is the only theme that can answer the big and mysterious questions of life: Where did I come from? Why am I here? Where am I going? Why is the world so evil if God is so good? Why do the innocent suffer?

The great controversy theme not only tells us how evil began, it clearly shows how it will end. It gives us the promise that sin and death will soon be gone forever and that we can have the hope of eternal life in a place of perfect peace and sinlessness.

The great controversy, finally, is the only framework that shows how each Bible truth relates to the others. Want to know how the truth of the millennium relates to the truth of the Sabbath? The great controversy theme will tell you. When seen in the setting of the great controversy, each truth takes its place like a single piece of a puzzle.

People love stories. Stories help people understand abstract things. And there is no story bigger, more important, more riveting, than the story of the great controversy.

4. The Spirit of Prophecy drives its readers to the Word. The Bible calls itself the Word—but it also makes clear that Jesus Himself is the Living Word. And if there was any reason more vital than any other that God gave this great gift to His remnant people, it was to drive them to both the Living Word and the Written Word.

The writings of Ellen White breathe the love and character of Jesus, the Word. Her great burden was to bring her readers into a deep, real, growing, and daily relationship with Him. She exalted Him in all she wrote. And knowing that since His resurrection, Jesus is perhaps more clearly made known in the Written Word than anywhere else, she also exalted the Bible as well. Her last public appearance before the church assembled in business session ended as she held high her Bible and said, "Brethren, I commend unto you this Book!"

5. Through the Spirit of Prophecy, God shared not just how to be happy and holy—but how to be healthy. One of the greatest gifts God has given His people through the prophetic gift is what Adventists have come to call "the health message."

Today, medical science and research continues to arrive at conclusions confirming what Ellen White said about health, disease, and the human body a hundred years ago or more. At a time when doctors prescribed smoking as a *treatment* for lung disorders, she warned against the deadly effects of nicotine. She proved decades ahead of her time in warning against a flesh-based diet, overeating, and alcohol. And today expensive health spas employ nature's simple and natural methods of healing—which she wrote about decades ago.

6. Also through the prophetic gift, God has shared timely instructions and predictions with His people. Early in her ministry, before it even began, Ellen White warned of the tragedy that would become the Civil War. She also prophesied the rise of spiritualism—which in our time has multiple manifestations: New Age philosophy, eastern mysticism, communication with the dead, astrology, psychics and mediums, and many others. Of particular relevance today are her predictions concerning the role of the papacy and the United States in the fulfillment of Bible prophecy.

Yes, if God indeed gave this great prophetic gift to His remnant people, you can be certain that the enemy will attack it aggressively. And he has. Every possible accusation and question and charge has been brought against it. Every doubt and insinuation possible has been raised. But just as the Word which it exalts still stands after centuries of attack, so too does the prophetic gift of God's remnant.

We Are Blessed . . . and Honored

Beyond all question, Ellen White was a fallible human being. She was subject to making mistakes, even as an author. But take the entirety of what she wrote, rather than isolated words or sentences, and you see that her message was—and is—consistent and sensible and in harmony with the "greater light."

Some Adventists seem at times a bit embarrassed that "we have a prophet." But was Israel embarrassed that they had a sanctuary, a temple, their own prophets—that they too were a "chosen" people? We should feel blessed and honored that God has entrusted this amazing gift to those of us in His final remnant.

God didn't leave us to find our way through the rocky channels on our own...He sent us a harbor pilot.

What does that say about us? And about Him?

*In every age, God has ALWAYS had a people—faithful and
loyal, the called and chosen—and He still has
a special people today.*

CHAPTER 13

WHO ARE WE?

S oon after the Great Disappointment of 1844, those who would lead out in what would become the Seventh-day Adventist Church could have all met together in the "parlor" or "sitting room" of a typical home of that era.

By 1863, when the Church officially organized, it had about 3,500 charter members.

As of 2006, world membership of the Church stands at approximately 15 million—and is growing in most recent years at the rate of a million new members a year.

This amazing growth is, of course, truly reason to celebrate. It's one measure of how successful God's "called-out" people have been in their efforts to win others to Jesus and His last-day truths. And while it's true also that Seventh-day Adventists are an officially organized denomination, they have never seen themselves as "just another church." Instead, Adventists see themselves as a "movement"—a people who exist because God not only prophesied they would, but when the prophesied time came, called them out of the confused "Babylon" of other churches to present His final messages to the world.

Adventists, like ancient Israel, are convinced they are an especially chosen people. But they know that being chosen doesn't imply that they are somehow spiritually superior to others. Rather, they realize that being chosen means they have a unique and urgent message to share with the world. Unique, because no other people on earth possess such a complete system of truth. Urgent, because time is running out as the second advent of Jesus draws near.

But if our stunning growth over the decades is good reason to celebrate and be grateful, it is also true that growth that is just random and chaotic can lead to disaster. Any doctor can tell you that cancer, by definition, is the disorganized, chaotic, and rapid multiplication of cells.

So throughout our history, we've had to organize, reorganize, then organize again. And before our mission on earth is over when Jesus comes again, we may see even more changes in how we're organized as a Church for service.

For certain, the way we organized ourselves in 1863 when we had 3,500 members just isn't adequate—it would be impossibly unworkable—today with 15 million members.

So as the Church grew, its leaders realized that to be most effective in carrying forward the mission God gave us, we needed to organize that work by smaller geographical units. At first, there was a General Conference—the central headquarters of our work. Certain states and smaller areas also had their "local" conferences. As the Church rapidly expanded, it realized that it would be far more efficient to group several local conferences into a "union" conference, so in 1901, union conferences were formed.

Today, we have the following "steps" or levels of church organization:

▸ The local church
▸ Local conferences
▸ Union conferences
▸ The General Conference and its Divisions

Divisions—which can include an entire continent, parts of continents, or island areas—are called "divisions," because they are considered to be "branches" of the General Conference in their respective areas of the world. Divisions are not separate, independent levels of church organization—rather, the divisions *ARE* the General Conference operating in their respective areas of the world. At present, there are thirteen world divisions:

▶ East-Central Africa Division

▶ Euro-Africa Division

▶ Euro-Asia Division

▶ Inter-American Division

▶ North American Division

▶ Northern Asia–Pacific Division

▶ South American Division

▶ South Pacific Division

▶ Southern Africa–Indian Ocean Division

▶ Southern Asia Division

▶ Trans-European Division

▶ Western Africa Division

Within each of these divisions are the union conferences and missions. The North American Division, for example, has nine union conferences—each of which encompasses various states, parts of states, or in Canada, provinces.

Each "level" of our Church exists to serve the other entities in its territory—to provide resources, administration, training, and spiritual motivation for them. Each entity—each level—of the church structure derives its authority from the representative and collective will of the constituents—or members—in that geographical area. The various levels of church organization are mutually accountable to each other for the accomplishment of their objectives—whether that level is the local church, conference, or union.

For example, the individual churches in a given conference are accountable to—and exist at the will of—the collective constituency of the entire conference. Just as the delegates to a regularly scheduled meeting of the constituency in a given conference hold the conference leadership and executive committee accountable, the individual churches in that conference are to be held accountable to the collective will of all the churches in that conference.

As an Adventist, you are likely already well acquainted with the structure of our Church, so it's not necessary to devote whole chapters here to lists of every local and union conference worldwide—or the history and role of each such organization in its area of the world. You can easily find such information in the *Adventist Yearbook* or the *Seventh-day Adventist Encyclopedia*—either the print edition or the online Internet edition.

But—and here is the important thing to note from our present discussion—you can be proud that just as an army is well organized to accomplish its mission, so is your Church! You belong to a Church that does its best to be efficient so it can produce maximum results. In this case, the results aren't huge profits for shareholders, or military successes. The results we seek are to bring together every possible human being on this earth with Jesus the Truth—and His last-day truths.

As you attend your home Adventist Church, you can also know that you are part of what has become a worldwide movement—that you have brothers and sisters by the millions all around this globe who believe as you do and share your vision of a "finished work" and the in-person return of Jesus!

Though the Church began in North America, its members and leaders from the beginning cherished a global vision for taking God's last-day message to the world.

In 1874, J. N. Andrews left America, traveling to Switzerland as the first overseas missionary of the Church. Soon Adventist missionaries were leaving to serve other nations and countries every year—only a few at first, but soon a rushing tide of men and women heralding the gospel in other lands.

Some of the other earliest overseas missionaries to follow in the steps of J. N. Andrews—many accompanied by their families—included such men and women as:

1874: C. M. Andrews; A. Vuilleumier to Switzerland

1875: James Erzenberger to Germany

1875: D. T. Bordeau to Switzerland

1876: D. T. Bordeau to France

1877: J. G. Matteson to Norway

1877: Mr. and Mrs. William Ings to Switzerland

1878: J. N. Loughborough to England

1878: Maud Sisley to England

1879: Mr. and Mrs. J. P. Jasperson to Norway

Beginning in 1880, the annual number of missionaries grew rapidly, so that soon dozens were leaving for overseas assignments every year.

Australia, the West Indies, India, Trinidad, Central and South America, South Africa, New Zealand, the Hawaiian Islands, Mexico, Polynesia—soon Seventh-day Adventist missionaries circled the earth.

Today, there is virtually no country—no remote corner of the earth—where the work of the Church is not moving forward. Perhaps no other Church on earth is so truly global as is our Church.

It's true, of course, that the onward march of evangelism—the progress toward that "finished work"—is not presently uniform the world around. In some areas, the remnant is growing like a wind-driven wildfire. So explosive is this growth that mass baptisms take place in large swimming pools—and new churches are being formed at an astonishing rate.

In other parts of the world, Laodicean apathy still persists. Affluence and overwork and the distractions of entertainment conspire to lull church members into lethargic inaction. People can only share their own experience and knowledge. And if their "first love" has grown cold and they no longer remember why they are Adventists, they have neither the interest nor the motivation to share anything with others.

But the good news is that in the end, the latter rain of the Holy Spirit will sweep through the entire worldwide church, bringing new passion and energy and vision—a new and overwhelming desire on the part of members to win others to the Jesus with whom they have renewed their own love relationship.

When that time comes, the growth of the church will be uniformly rapid worldwide. Evangelism will be truly global—and will move forward not alone by public meetings but even more so by the army of an ignited lay membership. Love is the most powerful force in the universe, and when it becomes the driving source of power for God's final true followers, the entire world will be confronted with a last eternal decision: loyalty to God and His truth—or loyalty to the enemy, primarily in the form of serving self.

A Worldwide Outreach

As you consider the worldwide outreach and ministry of your Church, think again of the many vital ways in which it touches people's lives. Around the world, Adventists are busy, active, involved Christians. This activity takes many forms—chief among them the following:

EVANGELISM—Through public meetings (particularly in recent years using satellites to reach a larger audience), personal Bible studies, literature distribution, radio and television broadcasts, health seminars, and other avenues, we reach out to our neighbors and friends to share the gospel of Jesus Christ.

EDUCATION—Adventists operate nearly 6,000 schools worldwide—from elementary level through college and university.

HEALTH AND MEDICAL—Over 500 Adventist hospitals, sanitariums, clinics, and dispensaries are scattered around the globe.

DISASTER AND FAMINE RELIEF—Through the efforts of the Adventist Development and Relief Agency (ADRA), our church is able to respond quickly to disasters anywhere in the world with food, clothing, and medical supplies. In addition, ADRA carries on a continuous program of famine relief in drought-stricken areas of the world.

COMMUNITY SERVICES—Many local Seventh-day Adventist churches operate Community Service Centers, staffed with church volunteers who assist the needy and homeless in their communities.

PUBLISHING—With nearly 60 publishing houses around the world, Seventh-day Adventists are totally committed to sharing God's good news with the world through the printed page.

COMMUNICATION—Adventists were among the first to bring the gospel of Jesus Christ to both radio and television. Today, broadcasts such as "The Voice of Prophecy," "Lifestyle Magazine," "Breath of Life," and "It Is Written" reach millions around the world.

It's wonderful to know we're a growing Church—an organized Church, a worldwide family. But we also need to be on guard. After all, the seventh and last Church of Revelation is Laodicea.

"And to the angel of the church of the Laodiceans write, 'These things says the Amen, the Faithful and True Witness, the Beginning of the creation of God: "I know your works, that you are neither cold nor hot. I could wish you were cold or hot. So then, because you are lukewarm, and neither cold nor hot, I will vomit you out of My mouth. Because you say, 'I am rich, have become wealthy, and have need of nothing'—and do not know that you are wretched, miserable, poor, blind, and naked—I counsel you to buy from Me gold refined in the fire, that you may be rich; and white garments, that you may be clothed, that the shame of your nakedness may not be revealed; and anoint your eyes with eye salve, that you may see. As many as I love, I rebuke and chasten. Therefore be zealous and repent. Behold, I stand at the door and knock. If anyone hears My voice and opens the door, I will come in to him and dine with him, and he with Me."—Revelation 3:14-20.

What do we need to guard against? A lukewarm spiritual experience. That can happen when our personal connection with Jesus is allowed to languish. It can happen if we get so busy we forget to keep investing in our relationship with Him.

What else do we need to guard against? Feeling self-sufficient. Being convinced we're doing just fine, when we aren't. And that can be true both of our own personal Christian walk—and the way we work together as a Church. Churches too can become self-sufficient, relying on their programs and plans and budgets and organization instead of on the only real Source of power—God's Holy Spirit.

But, the message to Laodicea says, we can repent. We can seek God's gold and white garments and eyesalve—His righteousness and love and His Spirit. And we can invite Him in as He stands at the door knocking.

Imagine leaving Jesus standing at the door without answering it! But we can be in danger of that—personally, and as a Church.

So as we think about what it means to be a part of the remnant—as we consider what being an Adventist is really all about—let us take seriously God's diagnosis of Laodicea's ills. Because *we* are Laodicea!

In college classrooms, good professors hope that from each lecture, their students will take home at least one important thought—the main point of the lecture. This book too has a "take-home" message. Here it is: You are a part of something BIG—something of earth-shaking importance, something that's a far greater priority than anything you'll ever hear about on cable TV news. You are a part—the final part—of an unbroken chain of God's faithful from Eden lost to Eden restored. You have a special role to play. God needs you—yes YOU—to find and use the spiritual gifts He has given you. He needs you to develop a passion for those who don't know Him as you do. He needs you to be available to Him every single day so He can reach others *through* you. God needs you to be His voice, His hands, His presence to those blinded by Satan's lies about Him. He needs you to tell the *truth* about who He really is. He needs you to let Him love other people through you. He needs you to let Him live in you so others can see His character of love "close up and personal"!

Our Identity

As we travel through life, each of us grapples with the great question of our personal identity: "Who am I?" Sometimes we confuse our identity with what we do, what we accomplish, or what others think of us. But you are unique. I am unique. Each of us is utterly unique. And it's important to discover who we really are, apart from our jobs, apart from the roles we play in life, apart from the opinions of others.

And if you are a Seventh-day Adventist, you also grapple with another great question of identity. Not personal identity, but our group identity. "Who are *we*?"

What is an Adventist? What are we here for? Why do we exist?

The *Encyclopedia of American Religions* reports on the beliefs of 1,588 denominations or faith groups in the United States. And the *World Christian Encyclopedia* identifies 10,000 distinct religions around the world. Just one of those religions, Christianity, includes 33,830 different worldwide denominations.

So as Adventists, are we just one more of those thousands of churches and denominations on earth? Is there really something special about this Church? Are we really a remnant haven into which God is calling the deceived and lost of Babylon's false doctrines? Are we truly a movement of destiny with the urgent message of a world about to end?

Yes, it's true, we as Adventists sometimes get distracted. We lose our focus. We end up derailed for a while as we fall into arguments about doctrines or church standards or whether the gift of prophecy is really still relevant. We see that the great enemy doesn't leave us alone. He attacks Adventist marriages, Adventist schools, Adventist institutions, and even Adventist leaders.

But friends, even if and as the devil does his worst, God is already doing His best. And we have yet to see the full power of the prophesied latter rain—the mighty outpouring of God's Spirit. The latter rain will provide *power* to God's people—unprecedented Pentecostal power for witnessing—but it will not *transform* them into the likeness of Jesus.

Revelation 7 tells us that at the end of time, God's people will receive the "seal of God": "Then I saw another angel ascending from the east, having the seal of the living God. And he cried with a loud voice to the four angels to whom it was granted to harm the earth and the sea, saying, 'Do not harm the earth, the sea, or the trees till we have sealed the servants of our God on their foreheads'"—Rev. 7:2, 3.

Foreheads: minds....hearts. Those who receive God's seal have so settled into their loyalty to Him and to His truth that they can no longer be moved—their commitment to God is irreversible. They have reached a place in their Christian walk where they would rather die than choose their own selfish way ever again.

This "settling in" process is steady and gradual—it takes place over a period of time, perhaps years or even decades. For some, it may be rapid, for others, less so. This process of settling into truth is perhaps something like how, slowly but gradually, freshly poured concrete "sets." Eventually, the concrete is solid and hard—and that hardening process can't be reversed.

Once God's people have "settled into" the truth—and into irreversible loyalty to their God—then....finally *THEN*....God can pour out on them His Holy Spirit in limitless power for a rapid finishing of the work He has entrusted to His remnant messengers.

Showing and Telling

And when God's people witness—when they share their faith—they are far more than just *proclaimers*. As any good writing teacher emphasizes, *showing* trumps *telling* any day! Spirit-driven witnessing is far more than sharing information—though it can certainly include that. The primary witness of God's people, however, is not just what others *hear them say*—but what others *see them live*.

At the end, God's people will demonstrate in their lives just how much power God truly has to change human beings when He is given an unrestricted invitation to do so. In their lives, God's people will demonstrate that just as Jesus could obey His Father by relying on divine power, so too can any of God's followers today do the same if they rely on God as Jesus did.

God is beyond eager to end the great controversy and all the heartbreaking misery it continues to cause. But Satan's false charge that God has made a law that can't be kept (his excuse for his own rebellion) must be fully met. So God will be patient enough to allow enough time—time for His people to answer in their own lives that false charge so utterly that it can never be raised again. We here on earth may be impatient for the end of the conflict. If so, by making ourselves fully available to God every day—by allowing Him to change us until we are sealed as forever His—we can help hasten the return of our Saviour and Lord.

In some parts of the world, the work of the Church is already racing through the populace like a wildfire through dry grass. One might rightly suspect that the earliest beginnings of the predicted latter rain may already be underway. In other parts, things are much slower by comparison.

But things are about to change.

The evidence of what's happening in the world around us should be a wake-up call. The environment is rapidly dying. Both freedom and security seem under threat everywhere. The trails of devil-inspired devastation crisscross the globe. Everything is converging on something so earthshaking it will put every other headline on the back page.

We would likely be stunned speechless if we really knew how little time we really have left.

Soon the final head-to-head confrontation of good and evil will dominate everything. And God's last, chosen, loyal remnant followers are going to be center stage when that happens. For the last acts in the drama, God may call forth His final Noahs and Davids and Luthers.

With the final wrap-up so close, what should we be doing *now?*

The answer is probably much easier to understand if you've ever been in love. Perhaps you've known the love of a parent or child or brother or sister or friend. Or perhaps you've known romantic love, marital love.

If you've ever experienced profoundly deep love, you know that you would do *anything* for the one you love. You also know that one of your greatest pleasures is telling others how wonderful your loved one is.

What should we be doing now? As we wait for the final showdown of the great controversy, what should occupy us?

Look again at the words two paragraphs back. If you are in love with Jesus Christ, you will do *anything* for Him. You are especially eager to do things you *know* He wants you to do. He wants you most of all to show others what He is like by letting Him live His life *through* you. At times, He may ask you to share what you know of His truth. He may even give you a special gift for teaching or preaching or sharing. But what He needs from every Seventh-day Adventist—and He needs it today—is for each of us to be His channels of love and blessing to others. He needs us to live out His character so clearly others can't miss it. He urgently needs people through whom He can show others what He Himself is really like! He will win His rebels back when they see His love demonstrated at *close range!*

When we are in love with Jesus Christ, we also aren't timid or self-conscious in the least about *telling* others about Him. Yes, it's true we have many truths to share with the people around us. But our first mission is to bring them to know and love the same Savior we know and love. Once they know and love Him, convincing them of His last-day truths will seem effortless.

The countless faithful and loyal from Adam's time to these early years of the 2000s stood firmly for the God they loved. They would not waver from truth   and they would not accept error even to save themselves.

Someday soon—undoubtedly far sooner than we realize—

we Seventh-day Adventists will have the privilege of meeting, on "the other side," the loyal who went before us. We'll ask them to share what it meant to them to stand immovably for the One they loved. And they will surely want to know what it meant to us.

Is there really any good reason to stay here longer on this planet of misery?

What do you say we give our all to finishing the mission God has given us?

What do you say we go home?

In every age, God has ALWAYS had a people—faithful and loyal, the called and chosen—and He still has a special people today.

CHAPTER 14

WHO ARE YOU?

You're a Seventh-day Adventist.

Maybe you were born into an Adventist home, went to Adventist schools, and have been an Adventist your whole life. Maybe you "found" the Adventist Church later in life and left behind your childhood church home to join this new one. Maybe you have only been a Seventh-day Adventist for a short time.

You're a Seventh-day Adventist.

Not a Catholic, Baptist, Episcopalian, or Methodist. Not a member of the Jewish faith, the Assemblies of God, or the Church of Jesus Christ of Latter-Day Saints. Not a Muslim or Hindu or Buddhist. Not an atheist or agnostic or deist.

You're a Seventh-day Adventist.

As such, you belong to a church that is like some others, but in important ways, very unlike any others. What other church believes as yours does about the significance of the year 1844? Where else do you hear anyone talking about the heavenly sanctuary and the investigative judgment—or "the great controversy"? And only few other Christians believe in the seventh-day Sabbath, the gift of prophecy in their midst, or the absence of consciousness in death.

You're a Seventh-day Adventist.

What does that mean to you?

How do you feel about being an Adventist?

In the long-running "Sesame Street" television program for children, the character Kermit the Frog sings a song entitled "It's not easy being green." Not when you're the only one who is, at least. Being "different" can bring ridicule and embarrassment and peer pressure to conform to the larger group. And sometimes, being an Adventist may not have been—may not be—easy for you.

Saying the blessing in a restaurant. Ordering vegetarian fare when you're the only one doing so. Running into resistance over your keeping of the Sabbath. Trying to explain the role of Ellen White and your church standards to others without being taken as "cultish."

You're a Seventh-day Adventist.

And as one, you have every reason to be proud (not boastfully or arrogantly, but because you're part of something unique and vital that God has created). You have every reason to share with others what you believe without embarrassment.

What does it mean to be a Seventh-day Adventist? Consider a few of many possible answers to that question:

1. To be a Seventh-day Adventist means that you are part of a movement God prophesied in His Word thousands of years ago that would appear exactly when it did, believe exactly what it believes, and have clear marks by which to identify it. It means that you are part of a people of prophecy—the "remnant" that would arise at the end of the 2300- and 1260-year prophecies.

2. To be a Seventh-day Adventist means that—no matter what the world's news agencies think is important—you are part of what GOD thinks is most important here in the early A.D. 2000s. You are part of His delivery system

for the final and most urgent messages God has ever sent to this planet. You are His voice—and your life is the demonstration—to those around you, that God's love and truth are transforming and the return of Jesus is imminent.

3. To be a Seventh-day Adventist means that you realize God loves this Church enough to give it every spiritual advantage, including the gift of prophecy—a gift that passes the tests the Bible provides to know the genuine gift from any counterfeit.

4. To be a Seventh-day Adventist means that you are part of a movement committed to restoring God's full spectrum of truths to this world. The truths recovered in the Reformation era, yes. But many other vital and unique last-day truths that will help men and women prepare for the return of Jesus.

5. To be a Seventh-day Adventist means you have the wonderful advantage of knowing how to be as healthy, as happy, and yes, as holy as God wants you to be.

6. To be a Seventh-day Adventist means you have a whole new way of looking at God's law—His commandments. You see them not as prohibitions to deny pleasure and plunge you into intolerable deprivation—but as God's loving directions on how to avoid ultimate pain and loss and finally, death. To be a Seventh-day Adventist means being freed from doing what the Bible says because you *have* to—to instead discover the joy of following God's way because you *want* to.

7. To be a Seventh-day Adventist is to learn by experience what "righteousness by faith" is about. Your Adventist view of salvation avoids "cheap grace" on one hand and legalism on the other. It avoids any imbalance between what God has done *for* you and what He wants to do *in* you.

8. To be a Seventh-day Adventist means that, unlike many other groups that simply go through the motions and have long since forgotten why they exist, you *know* why your church exists. Your church is here for a *reason*. You know it has a mission unique in the history of the world—a work to do so important that in the end, the entire planet will have heard the message of Revelation's three angels coupled with the message of God's love in the New Testament Gospels.

9. To be a Seventh-day Adventist means you are not part of a dying church—or even a church that is just treading water. You're part of a dynamic, rapidly growing movement that is a marvel to those who study church growth.

10. To be a Seventh-day Adventist means you're not a member of some small, regional cult. You're not anybody's "offshoot." You're part of a worldwide movement known not only for its growth, but for its global medical, educational, and humanitarian outreaches.

11. To be a Seventh-day Adventist means your church has its priorities straight. It hasn't wandered off—and never will—into politics and New Age theories and self-help psychology. Your church doesn't see its mission as legislating morality but in lifting up the only One who can create an inner moral code. Your church hasn't reinvented itself repeatedly. It hasn't changed its "product"—it has only one: Jesus and His truth.

12. To be a Seventh-day Adventist means understanding how your church—and how you—fit into the "big picture" of the ages-long great controversy between good and evil, between Christ and Satan. You are the last of the loyal, part of the final faithful, the end links in the unbroken chain of God's true followers through history. You are linked to all the faithful of the past: the

patriarchs and prophets, the chosen of Israel, the apostles and early-church believers, the persecuted of the early centuries, the loyal of the Dark Ages, the bold reformers of the Reformation, the energized Bible students of the Second Advent movement, the pioneers of your own church. You do not stand alone. You stand truly, boldly, proudly, unflinchingly, for the God who gave His only Son for you. You stand as part of God's last, indispensable people who know the urgency of so little time remaining—yet so many still to be introduced to their Saviour and His truth.

You are one of the remnant messengers who know the way to get off this planet alive and have both the mission and the privilege of sharing it with others.

You are a Seventh-day Adventist.

You are one of God's final chosen.

Embarrased? Timid? Ready to "hide your (peculiar and unique) light under a bushel"? Consider instead that the world desperately NEEDS what you have. So very many are looking to find what you've found. You are not odd. You are the one with the bread your fellow beggars on this planet urgently need. You are not weird. You are the one with the map to the gold.

Or are you afraid? Afraid—as you look back over the history of God's earlier faithful—that you may ultimately be persecuted? Afraid that you'll have to go through the Great Time of Trouble? Well, aside from the Bible promises that your bread and water will be sure—and aside from the awesome promises of Psalm 91—remember something else. God knows who will be able to endure not only persecution but even if necessary face a martyr's death. He will not call you to that unless He provides for you all that He provided for the persecuted of ages past. So cling to His promises not to fear. He does not want any of us to live in fear and dread.

Rather, focus in happy anticipation on the approaching end of this life's misery. Celebrate the imminent end of pain and tears and death. Prepare to abandon earth for an eternity of perfect peace, happiness, and the fulfillment of your every sinless desire.

You are a Seventh-day Adventist.

You are one of the last of the loyal.

You are part of the an unbroken chain of the faithful.

How fortunate—how blessed—can you possibly be?

In every age, God has ALWAYS had a people—faithful and loyal, the called and chosen—and He still has a special people today.

THEN . . . AND NOW

A few photos from the Adventist family album

William Miller (left) helped launch the Great Second Advent Movement in the first half of the nineteenth century.

The William Miller Chapel (right).

William Miller's home (left) on his farm in Low Hampton, New York.

Ellen G. White (above left—and with her husband James at above right), with Captain Joseph Bates (below left) were the founders of the Seventh-day Adventist Church. Mrs. White's son William C. ("Willie") White (below right) was a devoted assistant to his mother throughout her years of ministry.

Elmshaven (above) was the Northern California home of Ellen G. White in her later years.

In the late 1800s, Adventist physician John Harvey Kellogg, M.D., led in establishing the Battle Creek Sanitarium in Michigan. Center left: The Sanitarium as it appeared before a fire destroyed it in 1902. Bottom left: The Sanitarium, completely rebuilt, as it appeared in 1929.

In 1905, Ellen G. White, with the help of Pastor John Burden, led in purchasing a former health retreat located on a low hill in Loma Linda in Southern California (see photo above). From that humble beginning, Loma Linda grew into a world-renowned University and Medical School (see the main Medical Center/Medical School buildings in the 2005 photo below.).

In the earliest years of the twentieth century, a small dispensary was established on Boyle Avenue in south central Los Angeles, California. The medical outreach that began there has since grown into the sprawling White Memorial Medical Center complex (below), named for Seventh-day Adventist Church cofounder Ellen G. White.

The Seventh-day Adventist Church operates nearly 60 publishing houses around the world. This ministry started at the Review and Herald Publishing Association in Hagerstown, Maryland (right)—and continues at Pacific Press Publishing Association near Boise, Idaho (below).

The World Headquarters building (above) of the General Conference of Seventh-day Adventists—and the headquarters building sign (below). Photos copyright © 2005 by the General Conference of Seventh-day Adventists.